Life Together in the Spirit

Life Together in the Spirit

A Radical Spirituality for the
Twenty-First Century

John Driver

Edited by John D. Roth

This book is the 2015 selection for the
Global Anabaptist-Mennonite Shelf of Literature
of the Mennonite World Conference.

 PLOUGH PUBLISHING HOUSE

Published by Plough Publishing House
Walden, New York
Robertsbridge, England
Elsmore, Australia
www.plough.com

19 18 17 16 15   1 2 3 4 5 6 7 8 9 10

Front cover image: "Das Mahl" ("The Meal") from the Misereor Lenten veil titled *Hoffnung den Ausgegrenzten* by Sieger Köder © MVG Medienproduktion, 1996.

ISBN: 978-087486-696-4

Translated from *Convivencia radical: espiritualidad para el siglo 21* with permission from Kairós Ediciones. First English edition published in 2011 by the Institute for the Study of Global Anabaptism.

A catalog record for this book is available from the British Library.
Library of Congress Cataloging-in-Publication Data pending.

Printed in the United States of America

Contents

Prologue

Life Together in the Spirit is the seventh publication in the "Global Anabaptist-Mennonite Shelf of Literature," an initiative of Mennonite World Conference that seeks to promote shared theological conversation across the global Anabaptist-Mennonite fellowship. For many years, Good Books, under the gifted leadership of Merle and Phyllis Good, served as the primary organizers and promoters of the series. We are grateful now for the support of Plough in helping to move the series forward.

This text began as a series of workshops led by John Driver for pastors and church leaders in Latin America, a context deeply shaped by Pentecostalism. The book that emerged from those workshops, *Convivencia radical: espiritualidad para el siglo 21* (Kairos, 2007), reflected a deep respect for the gifts of the Pentecostal movement while offering a distinctive voice regarding the work of the Holy Spirit shaped by an Anabaptist theological perspective. In 2014, the secretaries of the MWC Commissions proposed that the English translation of the book – published in a limited edition in 2011 – be revised for inclusion in the "Global Anabaptist-Mennonite Shelf of Literature." Since then, we have simplified the text in some places, added study questions, and invited responses to the text from various leaders in the global Anabaptist-Mennonite church. We are pleased to offer it now to a wider readership in this revised form.

John Driver's name is well-known in Spanish-speaking contexts for the depth and clarity of his teaching. Even more importantly, Driver is widely recognized as a person whose very life – in his generosity, simplicity, gracious spirit, and evident love for all God's people – embodies the message of his teachings. In this sense, Driver reflects in his personal life what he yearns for in the church. That is, a witness to the living presence of the Spirit made known not because the church *has* a message, but because the church, in the quality of its life together, *is* a message. If the Spirit of the living God does not find tangible expression in the Body of Christ – if the good news of the gospel is not evident in transformed relations – the church is likely building on a foundation of sand.

In addition to expressing our deep thanks to Driver, it is a pleasure to recognize the important role that Steve Slagel, Greencroft Communities (Goshen, IN) and the Institute for the Study of Global Anabaptism (Goshen College) played in the initial translation and publication of the book. We are also grateful to Timothy J. Keiderling for his assistance with the study questions. Tim and Suzanne

Lind translated the essay by Mvwala C. Katshinga; Elizabeth Miller translated the texts by César García, Hermann Woelke, and Patricia Urueña Barbosa; and Elizabeth Miller and Phyllis Good assisted with editing.

May this text encourage Christians of all backgrounds, in every part of the world, to embrace a fresh understanding of the Spirit in all of its fullness, so that the Body of Christ may indeed be made visible in the world today. And may all who encounter that Spirit be transformed in every aspect of their life.

John D. Roth
Secretary, Mennonite World Conference
Faith and Life Commission

Foreword

One of my first memories of a Christian worship service
is of a Pentecostal evangelistic campaign one night in
Bogotá. My mother, who had come to know Christ
through a church of the same tradition, trusted that this
meeting – advertising healings and miracles – would be an
opportunity for my flat foot to obtain a normal shape, so
that I could finally walk without orthopedic shoes.

That night, at a young age – I would have been six years
old at this time – I looked at my mother with tears in my
eyes and told her that I believed that God had healed
me. From that moment on, I never needed orthopedic shoes again. God had worked in me the first of three
healing miracles that I have experienced in my life thus
far! Although the final two miracles occurred as an adult
in contexts of Anabaptist services, the influence of Pentecostal spirituality left an indelible impact on me, from the
early years of my faith. Many are the memories that testify
to that period of intimacy with the Spirit.

In other settings I have identified certain dangers that
I find in Pentecostal approaches that I do not consider to

be healthy – a tendency toward excessive individualism, for example, or the materialism found in the so-called prosperity gospel. Nonetheless, it is undeniable that Pentecostal spirituality has had a positive impact on many Anabaptist congregations in the present day.[1]

But Pentecostal spirituality is not the only type that has intersected with Anabaptism in the twenty-first century. The spirituality of the ecumenical Taizé Community and others from the Roman Catholic tradition are also valued by Anabaptist communities in different places around the world today. We need only cite as examples the impact authors such as Thomas Merton and Henri Nouwen have had on many of us.

As Dorothee Soelle has explained,[2] spirituality involves personal experiences, both individual and communal, that, grounded in faith, encompass human emotions and are therefore inherently subjective. Among the many varieties of modern spirituality how do we discern what elements are in harmony with or support our understanding of a life in the Spirit from our Anabaptist tradition?

Mennonite World Conference is not called to judge the validity of personal experiences in the field of spirituality. But one of the purposes of MWC is to strengthen our Anabaptist identity in such a way that it rests on the shoulders of our ancestors in faith while also being global, multicultural, and interchurch in nature. For this reason MWC has opened dialogue spaces where our member churches can experience communion, interdependence, solidarity, and accountability with one another. One of these spaces is the "Global Anabaptist-Mennonite Shelf of Literature," where MWC periodically selects and prepares a book meant to strengthen member churches in their common Christian faith.

It is within this framework that we present *Life Together in the Spirit: A Radical Spirituality for the Twenty-First Century* by John Driver. In this book the author invites us to bear witness to a spirituality that encompasses all aspects of our lives – a spirituality based on following Christ and adopting a distinctive set of attitudes, values, and actions before the world. This form of spirituality is not measured by material riches. Nor is it individualistic. Rather the spirituality described by Driver is experienced primarily in community and involves the sanctification of interpersonal relationships. Grounding himself in Scripture and in sixteenth-century Anabaptism, Driver reminds us that our ancestors demonstrated the truth of regeneration received by grace and expressed in the integration of faith and works, service and testimony, the personal and the communal.

In this sense, Driver does not look down on other spiritualities that can serve to enrich us in the present. Instead he invites us to value the richness of our own Anabaptist tradition with the hope that, even as we engage in conversation with other traditions, "we may continue to drink from our own well."

By offering this text to our global family – enriched by the study questions and the responses contributed by conversation partners from different cultures and Anabaptist traditions – MWC hopes that an Anabaptist spirituality will continue to develop in our time in a form consistent with our theological tradition and with profound respect and admiration for what other traditions contribute to our own.

Nearly five hundred years ago Menno Simons affirmed:

> True evangelical faith is of such a nature it cannot lie dormant, but spreads itself out in all kinds of righteousness and fruits of love . . . it clothes the naked; it feeds the hungry; it comforts the sorrowful; it shelters the destitute; it aids and consoles the sad; it seeks those who are lost; it binds up what is wounded; it heals the sick.

May the Spirit guide us as we grow in this type of spirituality – a deep, relevant, and challenging spirituality for our time!

César García
General Secretary, Mennonite World Conference
Bogotá, Colombia

Introduction

During the final decades of the twentieth century and the early years of the twenty-first, the theme of Christian spirituality has once again come to occupy an important place in Protestant thought. This has not always been the case.

As Protestants we had heard of Catholic forms of spirituality primarily practiced by the Trappist monks – known for the austerity of their lifestyle and their vows of perpetual silence – the cloistered nuns, or some of the other contemplative Catholic orders. With the general Protestant rejection of the Catholic orders that accompanied the sixteenth-century Reformation, we have generally underestimated, if not totally rejected, these and other similar expressions of Christian spirituality.

Instead, we have used terms like "devotional life" to refer to those attitudes and activities that nurture the inner dimensions of faith deep within our souls. We have tended to understand "spirituality" as a sort of inner, invisible energy that sustains and supports our lives as Christians in the world.

Not only has Protestant thought been dominated by this inward and highly abstract concept of spirituality; it has also tended to become almost exclusively individual and essentially private. Even our congregational spirituality – expressed in practices like common prayer, Bible study, and worship – has generally been directed toward the personal edification of individual members, rather than an integration of practices into a shared missional fellowship characteristic of an authentic community of faith.

The spirituality of the first disciples of Jesus, however, seems to have included all aspects of their life. In order to fully understand a spirituality that is truly biblical, we will need to overcome the false divisions we create for ourselves: that is, separating the spiritual, inner, and otherworldly from the part of us that is material, outer, and worldly. Christian spirituality does not consist of a life of contemplation *instead of* action, nor of withdrawal *instead of* full participation in the social order. Rather, Christian spirituality is the experience of every dimension of human life being oriented around and animated by the very Spirit of Jesus.

For this reason, we dedicate the first two chapters of this little book to a review of Christian spirituality during the first century. There we discover a holistic spirituality that consisted of following Jesus, under the impulse of his Spirit and in the context of a messianic community radically living out their faith together. It was a spirituality deeply rooted in God's grace, nourished and shared in the common life of the community of faith, and incarnated fully in its participation in God's mission in the world.

The third and fourth chapters describe the essential characteristics of Anabaptist spirituality in the sixteenth century. The Anabaptist movement was only one of many movements of radical renewal that have arisen throughout the church's history. Oriented by a commitment to Jesus and the example of the primitive Christian community of the first century, these movements have recovered to a remarkable degree – in their own life and within their own historical contexts – a spirituality amazingly similar to that of the Christian communities of the first century. In addition to the Anabaptists, a list of those movements could include groups like the Waldensians and the Franciscans of the twelfth and thirteenth centuries, the seventeenth century Quakers, the classic Pentecostal movement of the early twentieth century, the base communities within Latin American Catholicism of the past generation, and many more.

Finally, this brief study of radical spirituality concludes with a series of reflections on the possibilities for inter-church dialogue among the variety of spiritualities in the twenty-first century – reflecting a range of visions, convictions, and lifestyles – but especially between the present day heirs of historic Anabaptism and other traditions. We have the obligation to engage continually in warm and generous ecumenical dialogue with Christians from other traditions. We reject as false the idea that unorthodox belief or leaving the church is permanent or hereditary. Likewise, we reject the idea that authentic faith is automatically passed on from one generation to another. For that reason, our churches must always remain in dialogue with Christians whose history has been different than ours, and who have other ways of thinking and acting, even if their spiritual ancestors in others times and contexts may have persecuted our spiritual forebears for honestly held differences.

Study Questions

1. What is your perception of Catholic forms of spirituality? Why have Anabaptists often rejected them?

2. What has been our Anabaptist understanding of spirituality, in contrast to what the author calls "Catholic"? What is most important about Anabaptist spirituality?

3. How, according to the author, is the spirituality of Jesus' disciples different from spirituality as it has been generally understood by Protestants?

4. What do Anabaptists have in common with other radical Christian movements that have sprung up since the time of Jesus?

5. Why should churches – or fellow believers across denominations – remain in dialogue with one another? What is most important about Christian dialogue?

Christian Spirituality in the Gospels

As already noted in the introduction, the spirituality of Jesus' disciples touched every dimension of their lives. The biblical terms "flesh" or "carnal" and "spirit" or "spiritual" do not refer to two separate dimensions of human life – one outer and the other inner – but rather to two different ways of living, two orientations, two lifestyles. To be "spiritual" is to live every aspect of our lives inspired by and aligned with the Spirit of Christ. To be "carnal" is to be oriented by a very different spirit.

The community of faith in which Mother Teresa of Calcutta participated offers an example of a fully integrated spirituality. For her, "touching the untouchables" meant to "touch the body of Christ." To love in this utterly unselfish way was a form of prayer. One does not stop praying in order to serve; neither does one stop serving in order to pray. Authentic spirituality is "all-pervasive," affecting every area of daily life.[3]

This is the same vision we find reflected in Matthew 25, where the nations will be judged according to how they responded to the needs of the hungry, the resident aliens (that is, the undocumented immigrants in their midst), the poor, the sick, the imprisoned, and the outcasts in their land. To the surprise of all, Jesus reminded his hearers by saying, "Just as you did it to one of the least of these who are members of my family, you did it to me" (Matt. 25:40).

Recovering the Essence of Christian Spirituality

The cross of Jesus offers us the clearest model of an authentically Christian spirituality, reflected in the teachings of the New Testament. The cross is both a sign of complete identification with God and of total solidarity with the world. The cross reflects with absolute clarity the spirit of Jesus as well as the spirituality that his disciples would be called to imitate.

In this sense, the cross is the most eloquent intercessory prayer to the Father on behalf of the world. At the same time, it is the most energetic and convincing response of God to the powers of evil. Therefore, in the cross of Jesus – as well as in the cross that his followers are called to assume – we find the very essence of Christian spirituality.

Christian spirituality is the process of following Jesus Christ, animated by his Spirit, in the context of a truly radical (i.e., Christ-rooted) fellowship of faith experienced within the Body of Christ. This process leads into an ever-growing solidarity with Christ, in which Christians identify themselves fully with the life and death of Jesus. For followers of Jesus, the primary symbol of this living, dying, and rising again is baptism, by which we are introduced and welcomed into a truly Christian spirituality

(Rom. 6:4). This spirituality is marked by our following the Jesus of history within our own historical contexts. It is by the power of the living Spirit of Jesus himself, freely given to his followers, that this radical spirituality becomes a possibility.

It is a spirituality of the road.

Biblical Characteristics of Christian Spirituality

The New Testament offers the following descriptions of spirituality that provide guidelines for assessing the authenticity of any particular Christian spirituality.[4]

1. A truly Christian spirituality is based on the divine initiative of God's promise. The God of the Bible is the God who promises to save his people, freeing them from the powers of evil. No single historic expression of God's saving intervention on behalf of his people completely exhausts this divine promise. With thankful hearts we embrace every sign and symbol of God's transforming grace within human history that points in the direction of the kingdom of God. However, for Christians, these historic expressions are only partial and temporary. With Jesus, we continue to pray for the coming of God's kingdom in all of its fullness. Our commitment to follow Jesus must always be in anticipation of God's kingdom still to come in all of its saving glory.

2. This spirituality is an expression of hope. It consists of believing that which sometimes seems to be impossible:

namely, the reconciliation of humans among themselves and with God in a truly radical fellowship characterized by justice and peace. For this reason, joy is one of the principal characteristics of the messianic community – the community that trusts more in the power of God than in its own possibilities. This joyful hope fills followers of Jesus with the confidence and security that they need to live out the distinctive values of God's reign against the current of our culture. Within the economy of God's kingdom no effort that is aligned with God's rule of justice and peace will be lost (Rom. 5).

3. A truly evangelical spirituality implies solidarity with the suffering, death, and resurrection of Jesus. Just as Jesus lived and died – "the just for the unjust" – so also the salvation of the oppressors will come about through the nonviolent actions and suffering of the oppressed on behalf of the oppressor. It has been the experience of the messianic community that its salvation comes alone through Jesus' suffering on its behalf. Therefore, we confess freely that although the suffering, death, and resurrection of Jesus are truly unique in their saving power, they are not Christ's alone. In our innocent suffering on behalf of others we are "completing what is lacking in Christ's afflictions for the sake of his body" (Col. 1:24).

4. According to the New Testament, the purpose of the saving work of Christ is the restoration of communion among a humanity alienated from God and from one another. The restoration of relationships within the family of God requires the transformation of self-centered men and women into brothers and sisters shaped by a radically new fellowship of love. We experience this communion when we share our possessions for each other's well-being or when true authority is expressed in the form of mutual service (Matt. 20:25–28; Acts 2:43–45; 4:32–35). The example of Jesus, as well as that of the early Christian community, reminds us that authentic communion is characterized by a radically new understanding of the exercise of power, both in socio-political relationships and economic interactions.

5. *All spirituality that is authentically Christian will be characterized by this radical fellowship of love.* At stake here is not merely avoiding anything that might harm our neighbor, but rather actively pursuing our neighbor's well-being. To love as God has loved us in Jesus Christ is to offer our life itself for the neighbor in very concrete ways (1 John 3:16–17). The love of God, of which the New Testament speaks, is much more than merely God's love directed to us. It is also bigger than the love that we should have for God. At its deepest level, it is to love as God loves – that is, a willingness to lay down our lives for the neighbor in acts of unselfish heroism, as well as in the long process of yielding ourselves and our interests to the well-being of others in ordinary daily relationships.

A Spirituality Deeply Rooted in the God of Grace

A truly Christian spirituality is rooted deeply in the God of grace who has been most fully revealed in Jesus Christ. It is through the Jesus of history and his Spirit, that we can best know the Father, for Jesus "is the image of the invisible God" (Col. 1:15). Instead of speculating about the divinity of Jesus – based on the attributes systematic theologians have traditionally assigned to God – would it not be better to proceed just as the church in the first century did? They caught a vision of the invisible God before their very eyes in the person of Jesus and in the life he lived.

God has taken the initiative in our liberation from the powers of evil. God has first loved us! In reality, this has always been God's way of acting. The people of God were freed from slavery in Egypt, thanks to God's merciful initiative. Classical Protestantism has sometimes asserted that the Old Testament is characterized by the law and a righteousness of works, while the New Testament is characterized by grace and the good news of the gospel. But in reality, Israel was redeemed out of Egypt by grace and the people of the New Covenant are invited to live according to "the law of Christ."

It has always been God's intention to form a people in his image, a people that bears his name. Jesus not only teaches the character of God; he is also the perfect image of what God has always intended humanity to be. This divine project, which points toward the restoration of all creation to its original purpose, will culminate in the restoration of God's reign of justice and peace in every aspect of life. An authentic Christian spirituality is in complete harmony with this divine purpose and participates fully in its saving process.

As we know, the powers of evil and the dominant values of the fallen world conspire to distort the true image of God revealed by Jesus. We are prone to create idols that take the place of God. These idols lay claim to our loyalties, and we dedicate our time and our energies to them. But the God of Abraham, of Moses and of the prophets is a God who is active in human history, liberating his people from these false gods and the false loyalties that enslave us. In this, God was at work especially in the Messiah, who is the culmination of God's self-revealing acts throughout history: "No one knows who the Father is except the Son and anyone to whom the Son chooses to reveal him" (Luke 10:22). This is a God who is truly different from all false gods. Only an authentic Christian spirituality will be able to experience God fully and to show God's good news to others without twisting or distorting the message.

A Spirituality of Following Jesus

Since God has revealed himself uniquely and fully in Jesus, the way to know God is by following Jesus Christ (Heb. 1:1–3). Hans Denck, a radical reformer of the sixteenth century, said, "No one can truly know Christ unless he follow him in his life,"[5] a conviction that the heirs of the Anabaptist movement continue to hold. Therefore, following Jesus concretely is, without doubt, the most fundamental element of a truly authentic Christian spirituality.

Segundo Galilea, a leading Chilean theologian of the past generation, has expressed it this way:

> The originality and the authenticity of Christian spirituality consists in following a God who has taken on our human condition; who had a history like ours; who has lived our experiences; who made choices; who dedicated himself to a cause for which he had to suffer; who experienced successes, joys, and failures; and who yielded his life. This man, Jesus of Nazareth, is like us in every way except that he was without sin. In Jesus, all the fullness of God dwelt; so he is the only model for our life, as humans and as Christians.[6]

Lamentably, Christians have not traditionally thought about spirituality in these terms. Catholic spirituality, as well as that of classical Protestantism, has generally thought of the divine nature of Jesus as the Final Judge to be worshipped or as a sacrifice to appease divine wrath – but only rarely as a Lord to be followed in daily life. This has contributed to the emergence of a highly inward, abstract, and otherworldly spirituality.

Yet according to the vision of the New Testament, the words, deeds, ideals, and commandments of Jesus of Nazareth offer the only path to a knowledge of God

1. *"Blessed are the poor in spirit . . ."* A posture of spiritual poverty is fundamental to all Christian spirituality. Spiritual poverty consists of freely assuming the spiritual condition of being a child in the family of the Father. It is both the attitude and the practice of absolute dependence on God, trusting in God's providence as well as God's protection. It is that intimate relationship of utter confidence in God that Jesus himself demonstrated so clearly when he dared to call God *Abba* and taught his disciples to do the same.

But the Gospels do not permit an abstract or spiritualized understanding of this poverty. Sharing life together in the new community of the Messiah and living in radical dependence on God's providence cuts off all of our idolatrous and materialistic attitudes and practices at their very roots. "Choosing to be poor" (as the translation of the Nueva Biblia Española reads) in a world oriented in the opposite direction implies solidarity with Jesus – with the spirit and practice of poverty that he assumed freely and concretely in his mission in the world.

2. *"Blessed are those who mourn . . ."* Living out the values of God's reign in the midst of the world necessarily assumes solidarity with human suffering. It involves living in *sympathy* (literally, "to suffer together with") with those who suffer – indeed, freely assuming suffering on behalf of others. This innocent and vicarious suffering is absolutely central to an authentic Christian spirituality.

The Old Testament prophets spoke of the saving virtue that is found in innocent suffering freely assumed on behalf of others. But in Jesus we encounter the fullest expression of this reality. Our identification with Christ and our solidarity with fellow humans who suffer from all the various consequences of evil in the world calls us to take up the cross, even on behalf of our oppressors, with full confidence in what the resurrection of Jesus Christ promises to us – namely, that our innocent suffering for the sake of others will not be lost in God's salvific plan to restore creation.

3. *"Blessed are the meek . . ."* The meekness of the third beatitude is intimately related to the poverty of spirit noted in the first beatitude. It includes the inner strength that enables us to steadfastly resist the pressures of sin without yielding to its claims. It is the capacity to stubbornly resist evil without doing violence to the evildoer. This kind of meekness is rooted solidly on our hope and confidence in God. The meek person is one who truly believes that evil can be overcome with good. It calls us to reject the temptation to avenge ourselves with any form of violence or retaliation – to renounce all violence in the quest for justice and to struggle against evil with "clean hands" and a "pure heart." Far from being an ineffective strategy, this is, in fact, the strategy of the cross, uniquely and powerfully incarnated by Jesus of Nazareth.

4. *"Blessed are those who hunger and thirst for righteous-ness..."* Biblical justice consists of healthy relationships with God and with our fellow human beings in the context of a community that is absolutely dependent on the saving actions of God, both for its life together and for its very survival. Biblical justice includes the full range of interpersonal relationships and is anchored in the faith-fulness of God reflected in the common life of the human community that bears his name. This justice is visible only in the context of God's righteous (or just) reign.

Biblical justice, in contrast with what is generally called retributive justice, consists in giving people what they *need* rather than what they may *deserve,* be that reward or punishment. For this reason, we read over and over again in Scripture about God's justice for the widows and orphans, for the stranger in the land, and for the poor and oppressed. Authentic Christian spirituality expresses itself through our participation in the saving activity of God that leads to the restoration of just relationships among humans. It is within this community of salvation that the "hunger and thirst for righteousness" – just relationships among all – will be satisfied.

5. *"Blessed are the merciful..."* It is in showing mercy that we become most like God. The story of the Good Samari-tan provides us with a clear and concrete example of a spirituality characterized by mercy. To the degree that we are able to show mercy we will be in a condition to receive God's mercy for ourselves.

Mercy in the Gospels means, first of all, to forgive wholeheartedly in the same way that God forgives us (Matt. 18:35). In the second place, to be merciful is to unselfishly come to the aid of the afflicted and the needy. The limits of this mercy are not found in the one who extends acts of mercy, but in the capacity of the "neighbor" to receive mercy. What Jesus has taught us about the nature of mercy simply underscores the fact that a true Christian spirituality is characterized by our willingness to freely heap forgiveness upon our enemies and to share lavishly with the needy.

6. *"Blessed are the pure in heart..."* The "purity of heart" evident in all authentic Christian spirituality can probably be best understood in light of Psalm 24:3–5:

> Who shall ascend the hill of the Lord?... Those who have clean hands and pure hearts, who do not lift up their souls to what is false, and do not swear deceitfully. They will receive blessing from the Lord.

This purity of heart expresses itself in acts of integrity and in relationships characterized by faithfulness. Biblical spirituality is characterized by a close relationship between our inner attitudes ("purity of heart") and our external practices ("clean hands"). To know and to experience God is to obey and accompany God in his salvific actions, without divided loyalties.

7. *"Blessed are the peacemakers . . ."* Those who work for peace are children of God, especially in the sense that in doing so they are like their Father, who is the Peacemaker, par excellence. The God of the Bible does not rest in his efforts to restore wholeness, or shalom, to all areas of brokenness in creation. Jesus was fully committed to the restoration of peace – reconciliation with enemies occupied his attention throughout his lifetime as well as in his death. Activities oriented toward the restoration of shalom will characterize all authentically Christian spiritualties.

8. *"Blessed are those who are persecuted for righteousness' sake . . ."* The Beatitudes conclude with the innocent suffering of God's people. The spirituality that they reflect was countercultural, then as well as now. Persecution for faithfulness to God's reign of justice and peace was the lot of the prophets, it marked the fate of Jesus, and it continues to characterize the community faithful to its messianic calling. Biblically speaking, witness and martyrdom go hand in hand (*marturía* is the Greek word for witness).

When we remember that there have been more martyrs in our lifetime than in any other period of Christian history we recognize the contemporary relevance of the Beatitudes and their importance for our understanding and practice of authentic spirituality. This is true for the entire church, not merely for the church in the global south. The powers of death – arrayed as they are against

God and his intention for the restoration of justice, peace, salvation, and life in our world – remind us that the spirituality of God's people is inherently countercultural.

The spirituality of the Beatitudes is not an unattainable ideal, but rather a realistic and visible reflection of the Spirit and the words and the deeds of Jesus of Nazareth. The Beatitudes express the central values that characterized the life of the messianic community of the first century.

To follow Jesus is not a purely spiritual matter in the sense of being an inner or invisible reality in the life of the disciple. Rather, discipleship is a visible and concrete reality that expresses itself through the attitudes and actions described in the Beatitudes.

Study Questions for Chapter 1

1. How did Christians in the first century understand the terms "flesh" and "carnal" vs. "spirit" and "spiritual"? Why do we tend to view the physical and spiritual as separate dimensions of life?

2. What is so important about the cross? How is the cross, and the way Jesus died, an example for those of us who believe in him?

3. What should be our attitude to the future and God's coming kingdom? What does the coming of God's kingdom mean for our lives?

4. What does the New Testament say about how believers should relate to one another? How should Christians approach fellowship with each other?

5. Why have Christians often thought of Jesus only as "the Final Judge to be worshipped," as the author describes it? What is a better way to think about Jesus and the impact he should have on our lives?

6. What about the Beatitudes makes them such an effective summary of what life will look like under God's reign? What does each of the Beatitudes say about God's kingdom? How do they fit together?

A Spirituality of the Way

A Spirituality Rooted in the Spirit of Jesus

Following his death and resurrection, Jesus bestowed his
Spirit upon his followers. Since that time Jesus Christ
continues to be present in his Body, through the presence
of his Spirit. The Holy Spirit, present in the church, is
the same spirit with which Jesus was anointed for his
messianic mission. For that reason, Christian spirituality
does not consist only of following Jesus (who is the Way),
but also of sharing the life of Jesus (who is the Life),
empowered by the presence of his living spirit. Thus, a
truly authentic Christian spirituality is Trinitarian – a
life lived in absolute dependence on the Father, oriented
by its commitment to follow Jesus, whose life together is
permeated by the Holy Spirit.

The Old Testament presents the Spirit of God as the
source of life as well as the one who sustains the life of
God's people. The New Testament describes the activity of
the Spirit in the context of the creation of new life and the
ongoing sustenance of that life.

Likewise, the Gospel of John presents Jesus Christ as
the fulfillment of Judaism and the Jewish institutions
that sustained the religious and social status quo of the
period. Participation in the reign of God, now restored

by the Messiah, called for the transformation of Pharisaic
spirituality –the best that first-century Judaism had to
offer. As Jesus explained to Nicodemus, being transformed by the Spirit of Christ required that one be "born
again from above." The creation of a new humanity transformed by the Spirit of God was an essential element in
the prophetic vision of the coming messianic era (Ezek.
36:25–28). Thanks to the spirit that Jesus bestowed upon
his followers, the life that would correspond to the new era
(i.e., "eternal life") now became a possibility.

That same spirit – the presence of the Living Christ –
continues to sustain the common life of God's people. One
of the principal functions of the Spirit is to make clear
the teachings of Jesus in the faith community in order
to facilitate obedience in discipleship (John 14:26). The
Holy Spirit also inspires the gift of prophecy within the
community for discerning the paths that faithful living
will take (John 16:13). And in a very special way, the Spirit
enables the church to witness *(marturía)* with faithfulness
to God's reign. For its task of continuing faithfully the
witness of Jesus in the world, the Spirit encourages and
strengthens the church in its witness of suffering and
martyrdom (John 15:26–27; 16:1–4; Luke 12:11–12;
21:12–15).

Thus, the saving presence of Jesus Christ is continued
in the world by the Holy Spirit acting through the church.
The work of the Spirit embraces the entire spectrum of
Christ's saving work. It includes the creation of a commu-

nity of faith that bears the image of its Creator. It includes the Spirit's impulse to faithfully obey the teachings of Jesus. It empowers the followers of Jesus in their witness in the world, including suffering for the cause of God's kingdom. And it guides the church to glorify Christ through its experiences as a reconciled and reconciling community.

Scattered throughout the Epistles, we find a series of phrases that reflect the New Testament understanding of spirituality: "to walk according to the Spirit"; "to be led by the Spirit"; "to live according to the Spirit"; "to set the mind on the Spirit"; "to receive the Spirit"; "to have the first fruits of the Spirit"; "to be guided by the Spirit"; "to sow to the Spirit"; "to reap eternal life from the Spirit," etc.[7]

To live according to the Spirit of Christ is to take Jesus seriously as the model for our lives and actions. The Spirit, who is the impulse and the inspiration for our spirituality, is the Spirit of Jesus. In Paul's thought "spirit" and "flesh" are not two mutually contradictory human characteristics. Rather, they refer to two opposing spheres of human existence. One is the sphere in which human life is oriented by the Spirit of Jesus; the other sphere is a life opposed to God's restorative and salvific purpose.

Galatians 5:19–23 offers two lists of human characteristics that describe the fundamental differences separating the sphere of the spirit from that of the flesh. The lists are representative of a whole series of similar contrasts that we find scattered throughout Paul's writings (e.g.,

Col. 3:5–15; Eph. 4:2–3; 1 Cor. 6:9–11; 2 Cor. 6:4–6). The vices included in these lists probably reflect the areas in which the church's conflict with the values and lifestyle of Greco-Roman society in the first century was most intense. On the other hand, the virtues – or fruits of the Spirit – listed here wwere characteristics of Jesus, as he had lived among them: love, joy, peace, patience, kindness, generosity, faithfulness, gentleness, and self-control (Gal. 5:22–23). They saw these things in Jesus as they had never experienced before. These virtues are held up as models for creating and strengthening a Christian spirituality.

In all probability these lists were used for the instruction of new believers who were coming into the communities of the early church. Each of these virtues represents a concrete expression of the spirituality of the first-century communities. They reflect the firm conviction shared in the early church that the lifestyle and values of the kingdom inaugurated by the Messiah would continue to characterize the community of faith under the impulse of the Spirit of the risen Lord. Those who instructed new believers to follow Jesus in the way of his kingdom continually accompanied these new converts, walking with them in the presence of Christ's Spirit.

"To walk in the Spirit" meant to continue the life of the kingdom that Jesus had proclaimed in this new community of the Spirit. Jesus himself was the clearest model of what life in the new community was about. In him, the early church saw the fullest example of the fruits of the Spirit. And, as they understood it, the most crucial role of the Spirit was to inspire this ongoing fruit-bearing spirituality within the Body of Christ.

A Spirituality Nourished and Shared Within the Community of Faith

Christian spirituality is, by its very nature, experienced in community. The Spirit is present and active primarily in and through the Body of Christ, the church. Spiritualities that are completely individualistic and private lack biblical authenticity and will surely fail. Sooner or later they are destined to become mere ideologies or ethical systems. But a spirituality that is truly Christian – expressed in life together inspired by the Spirit of Christ – will be nourished in the church, which is a community of the Spirit.

According to the New Testament, holiness is essentially a *corporate* experience – saintliness is communal. The Bible does not recognize the concept of solitary sainthood or a purity focused strictly on the individual. When the Scriptures do speak of saints, almost without exception the term is used in its plural form. Indeed, the expression "the saints" is usually a synonym for "the church." Only within the communion of God's people is it possible to be "holy as God is holy" (1 Pet. 1:16).

The individualism that dominates the thought and vocabulary of the modern Western world has distorted the way we view the lives of those exemplary men and women of God in the history of the church. Instead of being the lonely spiritual giants that we often imagine, the saints were men and women who participated fully in the life and mission of God's people in the world. Their spirituality was nurtured by the same sources that God provides for all followers of Jesus through communion within the Body of Christ.

Therefore, Jesus can be followed authentically only in the company of other followers of Jesus. To follow Jesus is to walk together with our sisters and brothers in "the Way." This was one of the primary images the early Christians used to understand and communicate their corporate identity. The book of Acts refers to the messianic community as "the Way" at least nine times (9:2; 16:17; 18:26; 19:9, 23; 22:4; 24:14, 22). When we add to this the many occasions where the Gospels and the Epistles use this same metaphor to refer to the relationship of Jesus with his followers, we are confronted with an image of fundamental importance for understanding the essential nature of the church.

It would not be an exaggeration to say that the spirituality of God's people is fundamentally a "spirituality of the Way." Indeed, the image of "exodus" or "way" (*exhodos/ hodos* in Greek) plays a major role in the biblical understanding of salvation history in both the Old and the New Testaments.

Thus, the call of Abraham reported in Genesis 12 was, in a concrete sense, to participate in an "exodus" – that is, an invitation to follow Yahweh in his way. More than merely a geographic relocation, it called for a radically new spirituality. "I have chosen him, that he may charge his children and his household after him to keep the way of the Lord by doing righteousness and justice" (Gen. 18:19).

The liberation of Israel from Egyptian slavery was also an exodus, both in the literal sense and in a symbolic way. With a "strong arm" Yahweh redeemed his people, liberating them from their slavery in Egypt. But he also liberated them from Egypt itself and the imperial system it represented. Ultimately, the conflict was between Yahweh, the God of the oppressed, and Pharaoh, the lord of Egypt and the incarnation of its god. The newness of life for which Israel was liberated from Egypt was figuratively and literally a new spirituality of "the Way."

Subsequently, the prophet would see Israel's return from exile as yet another exodus (Isa. 40:1–11) in which the first exodus would serve as the foundational pattern for Yahweh's new redemptive initiative. Once again, prisoners would be liberated and Yahweh would be merciful to the poor (Isa. 49:8–13). Once again, God's redeeming action would consist in the restoration of an authentic spirituality of the Way.

References to the historical exodus abound in the Gospels, which repeatedly describe the messianic restoration as a new exodus. Thus, the New Testament presents Jesus as the "new Moses" who gives a "new law" from God on a "new mountain" to orient the spirituality of a "new

people" of God (Matt. 5–7). The Gospels describe the
death of Jesus, which was the culmination of an entire life
dedicated to the liberation of an enslaved humanity, again
in terms of a "new exodus" (Luke 9:31). And, undoubtedly,
the clearest image used in the Gospels to describe the
spirituality of this new messianic community is that of
following Jesus in "the Way."

For these reasons, the spirituality of the people of God
throughout all of their history has been characterized as
walking in the Way of God – the Way of liberation from all
the enslaving powers of evil; the Way that not only leads
to life, but is also the Way in which abundant life is already
experienced now. It is in this Way that we know and walk
with the God of our salvation (Deut. 8:2–6). The people
of God, according to the biblical vision, is made up of
"those of the Way." To know God, in the biblical sense, is to
experience God in concrete human relationships. We know
God as we follow obediently in God's Way. The spirituality
of this people of "the Way" finds its source, its model, and
its dynamic in Jesus, the one we follow in "the Way."

A Spirituality Incarnated in God's Mission in the World

The love of God for humanity has taken its clearest form in
the mission of Jesus in the world. We have witnessed this
love, not only in how Jesus lived but in the way in which he
laid down his life for others, especially for the marginalized, the alienated, and the enemies of God. In this same
way God's love is to be incarnated in the community of

faith (1 John 3:16–17). This is the way in which Paul imitated Christ (1 Cor. 11:1; 4:16; Phil. 3:17); and it is precisely this same tangible model that we are called to follow as "imitators of God, as beloved children" (Eph. 5:1–2).

The spirituality of God's people is to be expressed in every aspect of their lives. God's people imitate God – that is, they follow Jesus and they live out the communion of the Spirit – in all dimensions of life, both personal and corporate. To be sure, the presence of the living Lord in the world is experienced most fully in the life and mission of the church. But authentic spirituality builds relationships not only within the community of faith; it is also the impulse and inspiration for the church's participation in God's mission in the world. The same spirituality that nourishes the Body of Christ is also fundamental to its missional witness in the world.

The missional presence of Christ's Body in the world consists essentially in discipleship. Here again, Jesus is the model. Jesus' call to discipleship is an invitation to participate in the very same mission that God commended to his Messiah. To follow Jesus, who was "sent by the Father," is to share in the same vocation, characterized by the same spirituality, and by the same mission.

Matthew 10 briefly describes the mission of the apostles. Yet we should note that this was not a mission intended exclusively for the twelve disciples. In reality Matthew 10 reflects the missional spirituality that characterized the first-century community of the early church in which Matthew participated. Here we see that the whole life of Jesus – but in a very special way, his suffering and death – provided the ingredients for the spirituality of the original community that received the Gospel of Matthew: "A disciple is not above the teacher, nor a slave above the master" (Matt. 10:24).

To summarize: an authentically Christian spirituality is one that expresses itself in the mission of Christ. For that reason, it is a spirituality of the cross in the deepest sense: "Whoever does not take up the cross and follow me is not worthy of me. Those who find their life will lose it, and those who lose their life for my sake will find it" (Matt. 10:38–39).

Study Questions for Chapter 2

1. How does the Old Testament description of the Spirit of God compare with the New Testament description of what the Holy Spirit does? What do the Gospels tell about Jesus as the fulfillment of Old Testament Judaism?

2. What are the fruits of the Spirit? What kind of life produces such fruits?

3. Why is community so important? What in the New Testament specifically points us to community? What does the Bible say about sainthood?

4. How do the stories of exodus in the Old Testament point to the importance of sharing faith and living in community with fellow believers?

5. How does following in "the Way" of Jesus guide the life of the church and its mission in the world?

Spirituality in Sixteenth-Century Anabaptism

The Anabaptist movement of the sixteenth century inherited much of the monastic spiritual tradition of the Middle Ages, especially its understandings and practices that sharply separated the church and the world. But the Anabaptists rejected the long-standing liturgical-sacramental tradition as well as the hierarchical structures of the church and monastery. Instead, they promoted intensive Bible study in more family-like structures, in which their gatherings were held in their homes and their relationships were familial. They saw themselves as brothers and sisters. Here they developed a strong sense of a universal calling to Christian discipleship and mission, together with the exercise of the freedom of the will that this implied.

The Anabaptist vision was forged out of their experience of a fresh reading of the Scriptures in the context of their communities of faith. Rather than emphasizing the highly contemplative life of meditation and prayer, common among the Catholic orders, or focusing on right doctrine, as mainstream Protestants have tended to do, Anabaptists asked, "How can we be obedient to the gospel of Jesus Christ?"

Although medieval monasticism and Anabaptism held much in common, their different understandings of the Christian community, or the church, resulted in different spiritualities. Instead of an abstract or otherworldly mysticism, the Anabaptists emphasized the practice of obedience, active love, and the integration of faith and works. Their focus was not so much on cultivating a common spiritual life through contemplation, as it was practicing a life of prayer, peace, integrity, and humility in the context of radical communal social relationships. Theirs was a Christ-centered quest to know and worship God. Moreover, the spirituality of the Anabaptists was a gift of grace bestowed by the Spirit, not the product of human effort.

Although the Anabaptist movement of the sixteenth century was clearly diverse, few groups expressed interest in solitary contemplation, introspection, or ascetic practices as such. What did interest them was the prospect of "walking in newness of life," thanks to a regeneration experienced through the marvelous grace of God that expressed itself in the integration of faith *and* works, of the individual *and* the community, and of service *and* witness. The spirituality of the Anabaptists – especially among leaders such as Balthasar Hubmaier and Menno Simons, who strongly emphasized the written Word – was essentially centered on their experience of the Holy Spirit.

A Spirituality Inspired by the Spirit of Christ

All aspects of the Anabaptist movement were inspired by a profound understanding of the role of the Spirit in the life of the church. They insisted that the Holy Spirit's work in human hearts was crucial both for beginning and for sustaining a life of faith. Many early Anabaptists, including Balthasar Hubmaier, who was one of the least "Pentecostal" among them, spoke of three baptisms – a baptism of the Spirit, of water, and of blood (1 John 5:7–8).

The Spirit also played a fundamental and active role in all scriptural interpretation. In their biblical interpretations, the early Anabaptists were more "spiritual" and less literal than most of the other reform movements of the sixteenth century. Classical Protestantism placed much more emphasis on an objective, literal reading of the Scriptures, while the Anabaptists tended to give more importance to a subjective, inner, or spiritual reading of the text.[8]

By insisting on the powerful role of the Spirit in biblical interpretation, these simple, unlearned people were, in part at least, protesting the monopoly of an established religion and its restriction of the interpretation of Scriptures to the church hierarchy and its clergy. In the Catholic tradition, clerical authority focused on the sacraments. Within classical Protestantism clerical authority resided in the power of their academic knowledge.

Testimonies from Anabaptists in all regions where the movement took root, by contrast, unanimously agreed that it was impossible to understand the Scriptures fully without the baptism of the Spirit. For this reason, Lutherans often accused the Anabaptists of "spiritualistic anarchy," following in the path of the Saxon radical, Thomas Müntzer.

The debate between Martin Luther and Thomas Müntzer – the radical reformer in Lutheran territories especially noted for his spiritualistic tendencies – clearly illustrates these two positions. Müntzer assigned a preparatory, or instructional, role to the Scriptures in "slaying" the believer so that he or she might awaken to the inner Word and respond to the Spirit. Without the Spirit within, Müntzer insisted, one "does not know how to say anything deeply about God, even if he had eaten a hundred Bibles!"[9] To this Luther responded that "he would not trust Müntzer either, even if he had swallowed the Holy Ghost feathers and all."[10]

Thus, the Anabaptists did not identify the Word of God with the written Scriptures in a simple and direct way. Instead, they insisted that the "inner word," the voice of God's Spirit, gave authority and value to the "outer word" of the written Scriptures. The Scriptures were important for knowing the will of God, but not absolutely indispensable. In this, the Anabaptists differed with classical Protestantism.

Among the principles Anabaptists used for interpreting the Bible were the following: 1) the active participation of the Holy Spirit; 2) discernment in the context of the assembled community of believers; and 3) a desire for faithful and obedient ways to follow Jesus daily as his disciples.

Their dependence on the intervention of the Spirit in biblical interpretation meant that some Anabaptists' interpretations were not always as literal as many of their contemporaries in other traditions – and sometimes even their brothers and sisters within the movement – might have wished. For example, Anabaptists' opposition to the power and influence of priests and clergy, along with their affirmation of the basic equality of all the members of the community of faith, was based more on a spiritual reading of the Scriptures than a strictly literal understanding of the objective words of Scripture. The same could be said of the Anabaptist willingness to recognize the ministries of women in their communities of faith. On this point they differed markedly from the established churches of the period, both Catholic and Protestant.

Virtually all Christians in the sixteenth century thought that they were living in the End Times. The Anabaptists conceived of the era in which they were living as the time when God was going to pour out his Spirit upon all flesh. Because of this strong emphasis on the activity of the Holy Spirit, the Anabaptists were always open – to some degree at least – to the possibility of new revelations on the part of the Spirit, consistent with those appearing in Scripture. They believed that they were living in a radically new historical epoch, the age of the Spirit that would precede the end of the ages. This vision enabled them to interpret the suffering they endured at the hands of their persecutors as the "birth pains" they assumed would necessarily precede the end of history.

A Spirituality that Envisions the Church as Community

In their vision of the church, sixteenth-century Anabaptists differed notably from the commonly held understandings of both Catholicism and classical Protestantism. Catholicism defined the church as a "sacramental communion," or a community of salvation in which God's grace was communicated through the sacraments of the church. Classical Protestantism defined the true church by its proclamation of the gospel in its purity and the proper celebration of the sacraments.

According to both definitions, the true church was essentially invisible, made up of the elect, known only to God. The true church, in these formulations, was primarily a future reality that will be visible only at the end of time. In this, Catholics and Protestants alike perpetuated the Augustinian legacy that had emerged out of the church's conflict with the Donatists in the fourth and fifth centuries.[11] All that is really required for the true church to exist, according to this vision of the church, are the clergy carrying out their appointed roles.

In sharp contrast to this, the Anabaptists insisted that the true church is a concrete and visible community, the Body of Christ present in the world. To a considerable degree this visible, embodied church life determined the tangible forms with which Anabaptist spirituality was expressed.

In their definition of the true church, the Anabaptists often resorted to longer lists of characteristics than those identified by theologians in the established churches. Interestingly enough, it was Martin Luther who, without intending to do so, provided one of the earliest definitions of a "believers' church."[12] Luther's early understanding of the church included the following elements:

1. a community in which participation is free and uncoerced;

2. a community of faith and life;

3. a community dedicated to mutual edification and mission;

4. a community of mutual accountability;

5. a community of generous sharing; and

6. a community of the Spirit.

Menno Simons, the sixteenth-century radical reformer from the Low Countries, offered a remarkably similar list of characteristics. According to Menno, the true church was marked by:

1. "the salutary and unadulterated doctrine of [God's] holy and divine Word";

2. "the right and scriptural use of the sacraments of Christ";

3. "obedience to the holy Word . . . in Christian life which is of God";

4. "sincere and unfeigned love for one's neighbor";

5. "the name, will, Word, and ordinance of Christ . . . confidently confessed in the face of all cruelty, tyranny, tumult, fire, sword, and violence of the world"; and

6. "the pressing cross of Christ, which is borne for the sake of his testimony and Word."[13]

Among other things, these lists suggest that it is not a simple task to define the nature and mission of the true church. In the case of the sixteenth-century Anabaptists, the ecclesial symbols or signs with which they expressed their vision of the church provide a clearer understanding of their communal spirituality. These signs are baptism, giving and receiving counsel, the Lord's Supper, and mutual aid.

1. Baptism The term "Anabaptist" ("rebaptizers") was originally intended as an insult against the movement by their sixteenth-century adversaries. The Anabaptists themselves would have preferred a name like "brothers and sisters." But by their choice of "Anabaptist" their enemies correctly identified the fundamental issue in the debate.

The temptation among Anabaptists to spiritualize the sign of water baptism was very real – doing so would have meant the difference between life and death in the sixteenth century. Yet if members of the movement would have simply been content to emphasize only the inner baptism of the Spirit without the external baptism in water, the Anabaptist movement would not have survived. It was their persistent insistence on the necessity of this outward sign, together with the social and spiritual realities that it symbolized, that assured the existence of a visible alternative vision of the church that we have come to know as Anabaptism. For the Anabaptists, the inner baptism of the Spirit called for an outward and visible sign – water baptism.

For them baptism carried the following meanings:

1. a public confession of their sin, together with a declaration of repentance, in the presence of a confessing congregation;

2. a testimony to faith in Christ's forgiveness of sin;

3. an incorporation into the communion of the church;

4. a shared commitment to mutual sharing and to give and receive fraternal counsel; and

5. a commission to participate in God's saving mission in the world.

The early Anabaptists were the first church community in a thousand years – at least since the time of Constantine – to directly and explicitly relate the baptismal vows of believers with the missional vocation of the church. In contrast to the practice of the missionary orders within Catholicism – where the missional calling was limited to those upon whom the "orders" of the church had been conferred – the Anabaptists insisted that the "great commission" of Jesus applied to every member of the community by virtue of the baptismal vows that they had freely assumed.

Water baptism was also a sign of submission or "yieldedness" to Christ *(Gelassenheit)*. Included in the concept of yieldedness, borrowed from late medieval Catholic mysticism, were the following themes: 1) an inner commitment to Christ and his cause; 2) a commitment to the Body of Christ, the church, with all that one is and all that one possesses: "Be subject to one another out of reverence for Christ"(Eph. 5:21); and 3) a commitment to suffer for the love of Christ and for one's brothers and sisters.

Baptism meant a transfer of one's citizenship in this world, with its values and loyalties, to citizenship in another world – the Body of Christ, the church, with its distinctive set of values and loyalties. It meant a fundamental change of kingdoms and of lords.

When authorities interrogated imprisoned Anabaptists about the reasons for their baptism the response was generally quite simple. They baptized out of obedience to the biblical order in which belief comes *before* baptism – "The one who believes and is baptized will be saved" (Mark 16:16); "Repent and be baptized . . . so that your sins may be forgiven" (Acts 2:38).

For the Anabaptists, baptism was fundamentally a public commitment entered into freely before the community of believers. This commitment was the basis for their promise to follow Jesus faithfully in the context of the community of believers. Thus, baptism was the outward sign of an inner transformation and a public commitment to follow Christ. The "obedience of faith" it symbolized included not only the inner testimony of the Spirit, but also an outward testimony and commitment to a new life in community, entered into together with other brothers and sisters who had made the same vows.

The Anabaptist understanding of salvation was therefore essentially corporate – social and relational rather than simply an inner and personal matter focused purely on the individual. For them, the true church was a visible community characterized by outward signs of an inward transformation. Thanks to their insistence that inner spiritual realities could not be separated from their outward expressions, Anabaptism became a social movement.

2. *Counsel and Discipline in Community*

Sixteenth-century Anabaptists understood the teachings of Jesus in Matthew 18:15–20 regarding disagreements in the community to be an evangelical, nonviolent, and compassionate alternative to the traditional manner of dealing with conflicts. In sixteenth-century society, conflicts were resolved either by the state, in the exercise of its power to impose physical punishment, or by the established churches, in their power to punish offenders by imposing religious penalties or by turning them over to the secular powers for punishment.

The sixteenth-century Anabaptists' approach to correcting or punishing the wrongdoer was very different, although their spiritual heirs have not always been consistent in practice. From the Anabaptist perspective, the church's discipline consisted primarily in helping each brother or sister truly become the disciple of Jesus that they affirmed in their baptismal vows. The visible similarities between the terms "disciple" and "discipline" further underscore the logic of this connection.

For the sixteenth-century Anabaptists the restoration of the true church would not be complete until its members had freely committed themselves, through their baptism, to become this kind of community, sustained by the practice of community-based restorative discipline.

The purpose of this approach to discipline was not punitive or aimed at excluding the offender, but rather an expression of authentic evangelization. According to Balthasar Hubmaier, the offender was to be received again "joyfully, like a father receives a lost son" (Luke 15:20–24).[14]

For this kind of discipline to function, the congregation needed to agree that a person's outward actions were a faithful reflection of their inward condition. If a saving faith is, in its essence, known only to God, it would be invisible. Therefore, it would not make sense to exercise mutual discipline. But if we believe that the inner and the outer expressions of human experience and action are two sides of the same coin, the exercise of mutual discipline can be truly restorative.

The practice of Anabaptist discipline replaced the traditional ritual of confession, contrition, penitence, and absolution within Catholicism. Lutherans, for their part, hoped that the proclamation of the Word in its purity would have this effect. In contrast to both Catholic and Protestant understandings, Anabaptists believed that outward actions faithfully reflect inner commitments and therefore called for mutual accountability.

Viewed from a congregational perspective, discipline can be understood as the concrete form that the grace of God takes in the process of continually restoring wholeness to relationships within the community of faith.

3. The Lord's Supper The Anabaptists understood the Lord's Supper as a commemoration of the sacrificial death of Christ. In this they were the ideological heirs of a deep medieval anti-sacramental tradition expressed most vigorously in the sixteenth century by the humanist Desiderius Erasmus and the Swiss reformer, Ulrich Zwingli. But this basic understanding by no means exhausts the meaning of this symbol for the Anabaptists.

Even before the formal beginnings of the Anabaptist movement, dissidents in Switzerland – inspired initially by Zwingli's program of reforms, but then frustrated by his compromise with the civil authorities in putting those reforms into practice – had formulated some ideas that would radically "desacralize" the Lord's Supper.

Some four months before the first Anabaptist baptisms in January of 1525, several of Zwingli's closest disciples had referred to the celebration of the Lord's Supper in the following terms:

> Ordinary bread ought to be used, without idols and additions. . . . An ordinary drinking vessel too ought to be used. . . . Although it is simply bread, yet if faith and brotherly love precede it, it is to be received with joy. Since it is used in the church, it is to show that we are truly one bread and one body, and that we are and wish to be true brethren with one another. . . . [We] should be willing to live and suffer for the sake of Christ and the brethren. . . . The supper is an expression of fellowship, not a Mass and sacrament. . . . Neither is it to be used in "temples" . . . since that creates a false reverence. It should be used much and often.[15]

For his part, Balthasar Hubmaier wrote:

> Whoever now observes the Supper of Christ . . . and regards the suffering of Christ in firm faith, the same will also thank God for this grace and goodness and will surrender himself to the will of Christ, which is what he has done for us. We also now should make our life, body, material goods, and blood available to the neighbor. That is the will of Christ.[16]

This strong emphasis on horizontal relationships was widely held among the Anabaptists. We find a similar interpretation in the *Congregational Order* of 1526, an outline of worship that likely originated in the circles associated with Michael Sattler:

> The Lord's Supper shall be held, as often as the brothers are together, thereby proclaiming the death of the Lord, and thereby warning each one to commemorate how Christ gave his life for us and shed his blood for us, that we might also be willing to give our body and life for Christ's sake, which means for the sake of all the brothers.[17]

A common English translation of the central texts related to the Lord's Supper reads as follows: ". . . 'This is my body that is broken for you. *Do this* in remembrance of me.' In the same way he took the cup also, after supper, saying, 'This cup is the new covenant in my blood. *Do this,* as often as you drink it, in remembrance of me'" (1 Cor. 11:24–25 and Luke 22:19). We have traditionally imagined that "do this" simply referred to the practice of celebrating the Lord's Supper – that is, eat bread and drink from my cup. In contrast to this interpretation, the translation offered by the Nueva Biblia Española of 1 Corinthians 11:23–24 provides a clearer understanding of the texts: "This is my body, that is given for you; do *the same* in my memory" – that is, imitate me in this act of self-sacrificing love. Those of us accustomed to traditional interpretations of the Lord's Supper may be surprised by this translation. However, it agrees perfectly with the radical Anabaptist understanding of the Lord's Supper that we have just noted. Early Anabaptists, as well as the early Christian church, understood that both the practice of the Lord's Supper and a readiness to give ourselves on behalf of others were essential to the church's ongoing life.

In water baptism we testify to the fact that we have taken seriously the biblical command to love God above all else – that we have died to ourselves and have risen to newness of life in Christ Jesus. In the Lord's Supper we also give testimony to the fact that we have taken seriously the biblical command to love our neighbor as ourselves. This horizontal orientation of the Lord's Supper – as a response to the grace of God and as a commitment to love as God loves – is distinctly Anabaptist.

4. *Mutual Aid* From the very beginnings of the Anabaptist movement, participation in the Body of Christ implied absolute loyalty to Christ in our social, economic, and political relationships, which, of course, are also spiritual matters in the context of the community of faith.

Life within Anabaptist communities was inspired and enabled by the Spirit of Christ and ordered according to the model of Jesus and his disciples. It also meant that economic relationships among sixteenth-century Anabaptists would be different from those of the world. Among the Hutterian Brethren, for example, economic relationships were structured systematically around the principle of shared possessions, or a community of goods. Economic relationships among the Swiss and South German communities were less formally structured, but no less real. Both groups affirmed the same commitment to mutual aid, the same attitude of detachment from material possessions, and the same motivating Spirit. And both groups were judged by civil authorities to be a threat to the socio-economic system and were persecuted as danger-ously "seditious" and "fanatical," among other charges.

Article 5 of the "Congregational Order" summarizes economic relationships among the Swiss and South German Anabaptist communities:

> Of all the brothers and sisters in this congregation none shall have anything of his own, but rather, as the Christians in the time of the apostles, hold all things in common and especially store up a common fund from which aid can be given to the poor, according as each will have need, and as in the apostles' time permit no brother to be in need.[18]

The Anabaptists also rejected the traditional status distinctions that characterized sixteenth-century society. They abandoned the use of honorary titles in referring to each another, including those who exercised some form of ministry within the communities. A letter by Conrad Grebel to Thomas Müntzer, written in September of 1524, reflects this conviction:

Dear Brother Thomas: For God's sake do not marvel that we address you without title and request you like a brother to communicate with us by writing, and that we have ventured, unmasked and unknown to you, to open communications between us. God's Son, Jesus Christ, . . . bids us be brethren by the one common word given to all brethren and believers. [He] has moved us and compelled us to make friendship and brotherhood.[19]

Müntzer, like Grebel, held a master's degree, but the Anabaptists intentionally avoided honorary titles in referring to one another, since doing so would have perpetuated the social distinctions that separated the clergy from the laity as well as the educated from the uneducated.

Study Questions for Chapter 3

1. What did Anabaptists in the sixteenth century share with the monastic spiritual tradition? What, specifically, did they reject from Catholicism?

2. For the Anabaptists, what changed in their understanding of the role of the Spirit in the life of the church? What were some of the effects of this change?

3. How did biblical interpretation among sixteenth-century Anabaptists differ from other Christians of their day? What key concepts did the Anabaptists emphasize?

4. According to the author, most Christians in the sixteenth century thought that they were living in the End Times. How did this attitude affect how Anabaptists viewed their own faith?

5. What is so important about baptism? Why did the Anabaptists hold on to it, often at the cost of their lives? What were some of the meanings that sixteenth-century Anabaptists attached to the symbol of baptism with water, as opposed to "inner baptism"?

6. Describe the importance of discipline in the Anabaptist churches. Why was discipline – and the idea of discipleship in community as a constant process of renewal – key to the survival of the Anabaptist churches?

7. According to the author, Anabaptists rejected the Catholic tendency to celebrate the Lord's Supper as a sacrament. How did the Anabaptist understanding and practice of the Lord's Supper differ?

8. How did community among believers express itself in daily life for the Anabaptists? What did they emphasize about economic and social life that set them apart from other Christian traditions?

A Spirituality of Discipleship

A Christ-Centered Spirituality

As with many other renewal movements throughout the church's history, the person of Jesus Christ was central to the spirituality of sixteenth-century Anabaptists. Virtually all of their doctrine was consistent with the beliefs expressed in the historic creeds of Christendom. However, one important dimension of Anabaptist Christology, not emphasized in the mainstream tradition of the established churches, was the significance of Jesus as a model to be followed in daily life. In this the Anabaptists attempted to recover the reality of Christ's humanity, expressed in his words and actions, without ignoring or neglecting his divine nature.

Despite some early tendencies – especially in the Netherlands – toward Docetism (the idea that Jesus in his suffering only appeared to be human) and Monophysitism (the idea that Jesus had only one nature, the divine), the Anabaptist movement was characterized by a Christology strongly rooted in the Incarnation. They understood Jesus as both fully human and fully divine. From this emerged a spirituality of discipleship.

In contrast to sixteenth-century Catholics and the classical Protestant tradition, the Anabaptists resisted the temptation to separate law from gospel, or sanctification from justification, or faith from works, or discipleship from evangelization. In a context that understood Jesus primarily as "the Savior who dies" or as "the coming Judge," the Anabaptists confessed Jesus as "the Lord to be followed."

This commitment to following Jesus – a conviction based on an incarnational Christology – had more in common with earlier radical renewal movements, both within and outside the Catholic Church, than it did with the emerging Protestantism of its day. The Anabaptist commitment to imitating Jesus was similar to that of the early Franciscans and the Waldensians of the twelfth century and to the Czech Brethren of the fifteenth century.

However, the Anabaptists expressed a deepening of this conviction in both vision and practice. In addition to imitating Jesus in concrete (and sometimes legalistic) ways, the Anabaptists understood their ethical decisions to be directed by the Spirit of Christ. This understanding of discipleship as *participation* in the very nature of Jesus meant: 1) that radical discipleship would be possible, since Jesus himself had lived it out; and 2) that the words of Jesus had an authoritative meaning since Jesus himself had incarnated them. Therefore, a radically Christian life was not an impossible ideal – as sixteenth-century Christendom generally held – but a real possibility.

This "spirituality of discipleship" assigned great importance to biblical teachings such as the Sermon on the

Mount (Matt. 5–7) and the fruits of the Spirit (Gal. 5:13–
26), in contrast to other movements, which tended to
regard these passages as "law." For the Anabaptists, following Jesus in radical discipleship was the concrete expression
of their experience of God's grace in their midst.

A Spirituality of Justice and Peace

In their desire to follow Jesus, the majority of the Anabaptists committed themselves to a nonviolent path of
love and peace. They found nothing in the New Testament
to justify their participation in the wars of their time
or in other forms of coercive violence. For this reason,
with few exceptions, they were hesitant to participate in
the political structures of their day. Most believed in the
reality of two distinct kingdoms: the kingdom of this
world, which operates in conditions of sin, violence, and
human law; and the kingdom of Christ characterized by
grace and the gospel, and expressed most clearly by the
qualities of life in the community of faith.

In the sixteenth century many Anabaptists were persecuted and suffered injustices of all kinds. Nevertheless,
they generally enjoyed popular support, although this was
often hidden out of fear of the civil authorities. They were
pioneers in the struggle for human rights in economics,
as well as in their opposition to broader forms of violence
and oppression in their time, such as social hierarchies,
feudal inequalities, economic oppression, warfare, and the
death penalty. The implications of the gospel in questions

of justice, peace, and "nonresistance" – as they were accustomed to calling it, taking their cue from the term that appears in Jesus' teaching: "Do not resist an evildoer" (Matt. 5:39) – were not equally evident to all Anabaptists at the beginning of the movement. However, many quickly realized the importance of the Sermon on the Mount for their lives. The following citations are representative of early Anabaptist thought and action.

The first comes from Conrad Grebel and his circle. It is part of a letter dated September 5, 1524, addressed to Thomas Müntzer, a German mystic and revolutionary living in territories under the control of Lutheran authorities. For Grebel and his friends the church was to be established on nothing more or less than the principles of "the rule of Christ" (Matt. 18:15–20). This meant that coercion had no place within the community of faith. Whereas dissidents within the established churches were judged, condemned, and turned over to the secular authorities for torture, imprisonment, and execution, Grebel urged Müntzer to use only "determination and common prayer and decision according to faith and love, without command or compulsion."[20] "Moreover," he continued,

> the gospel and its adherents are not to be protected
> by the sword, nor are they thus to protect themselves,
> which, as we learn from our brother, is your opinion
> and practice. True Christian believers are sheep
> among wolves, sheep for the slaughter; they must be

baptized in anguish and affliction, tribulation, persecution, suffering and death; they must be tried with fire, and must reach the fatherland of eternal rest, not by killing their bodily enemies, but by mortifying their spiritual enemies. Neither do they use the worldly sword or war, since all killing has ceased with them – unless, indeed, we would still be in the old law. And even there [in the Old Testament], so far as we recall, war was a misfortune after they had once conquered the Promised Land.[21]

This same vision was confirmed almost three years later in an Anabaptist synod held in the Swiss village of Schleitheim on February 24, 1527.

We have been united as follows concerning the sword. The sword is an ordering of God outside the perfection of Christ. It punishes and kills the wicked, and guards and protects the good. . . . But within the perfection of Christ only the ban is used for the admonition and exclusion of the one who has sinned, without the death of the flesh, simply the warning and the command to sin no more. Now many, who do not understand Christ's will for us, will ask whether a Christian may or should use the sword against the wicked for the protection and defense of the good, or for the sake of love. [Here the "just war" is in view.] The answer is unanimously revealed: Christ teaches and commands us to learn from him, for he is meek and lowly of heart and thus we shall find rest for our souls. . . . The weapons of their battle and warfare are carnal and only against the flesh, but the weapons of Christians are spiritual, against the fortification of the devil. The worldly are armed with steel and iron, but Christians are armed with the armor of God, with truth, righteousness, peace, faith, salvation, and with the Word of God.[22]

Only three months after the Anabaptist meeting at Schleitheim, Michael Sattler, one of the principal participants, was judged and sentenced to an unimaginably cruel form of torture and execution. The list of the charges against Sattler provides a glimpse of the Anabaptist attitude regarding civil authority and the various forms of human violence.

1) That he and his associates have acted against the imperial mandate. . . ; 6) [He] said that one should not swear to the government. . . ; 9) He has said: "If the Turk were to come into the land, one should not resist him," and, "if it were right to wage war, [he] would rather go to war against the Christians than against the Turks," which is after all a great offense, to take the side of the greatest enemy of our holy faith against us.[23]

Later, in his own defense, Michael Sattler added:

If the Turk comes, he should not be resisted, for it stands written: thou shalt not kill. We should not defend ourselves against the Turks or our other persecutors, but with fervent prayer should implore God that he might be our defense and our resistance. As to the saying that if waging war were proper I would rather take the field against the so-called Christians who persecute, take captive, and kill true Christians, than against the Turks, this was for the following reason: the Turk is a genuine Turk and knows nothing of the Christian faith. He is a Turk according to the flesh. But you claim to be Christians, boast of Christ, and still persecute the faithful witnesses of Christ. Thus you are Turks according to the Spirit.[24]

Menno Simons, who provided the leadership essential to the survival of the Anabaptist movement in the Netherlands during the decades following a violent and disastrous uprising of Anabaptists in Münster in 1535, provides testimony in his writings on justice, peace, and nonviolence that is very similar to that which we have noted in the Swiss and South German movement.

No, dear sirs, no, [bloodshed] will not be able to free you in the judgment day of God (Luke 22:49–51). . . . They know no other weapons except patience, hope, silence, and God's Word (Matt. 10:14; Isa. 30:15). The weapons of our knighthood, says Paul, are not fleshly but mighty before God to destroy all attacks, over-throwing everything which lifts itself up against the knowledge of God, and taking all understanding captive to the obedience of Christ (2 Cor. 10:4–5).[25]

Nor did Menno Simons hesitate to bear witness to civil authorities who claimed to be Christians:

> I agree wholeheartedly that the office of magistrate is of God and his order. But I hate those who are Christian, and want to be one, and then do not follow their prince, head, and leader, Christ, but cover and clothe their unrighteousness, wickedness, pomp, pride, avarice, greed, and tyranny with the name of magistrate. For those who are Christian must follow the Spirit, Word, and example of Christ, whether they are emperor, king, or whoever.[26]

In the early 1530s Jacob Hutter emerged as a leader among the pacifist Anabaptist community in Moravia. The ruling nobles were generally well-disposed toward the Anabaptists, thanks to the economic benefits they brought to their territories, and were willing to grant them favors and protect them in the face of imperial decrees ordering their persecution. However, Hutter was resolute in his resistance to the nobles when they ordered the Anabaptists to pay taxes in order to finance the empire's wars against the Turks.

> Therefore [God] has also arranged that every government collect annual taxes or interest or rent that they may be able to carry on their office, and if someone would resist this, they would be found against the order of God. . . . Therefore we too have never resisted this,

as obedient subjects of human ordinances, for the sake of the Lord. However, where one departs from this order and against God, or not ordered by God, and seeks annual taxes for war or hangman's pay or other things which are not proper for a Christian or have no basis in Scripture, but rather are against God and his Son, to that we cannot consent. [Christ] did not come to condemn souls but to save them, not to return evil for evil, or blow for blow, but rather to repay evil with good, to show the nature of our Father in heaven by doing good to our enemies.[27]

In a document from 1642, the Anabaptists clearly declared that these principles of peace and nonviolence should be applied to the full range of human relationships.

One [should] always act toward the poor as one would have God act toward us. . . . Often persons are so harsh toward a neighbor, when they are to forgive them something, asking for a great confession of guilt before they can be forgiven. When they divide an inheritance, they are so shrewd that they want to make certain to receive their own share and not be generous simply for the sake of peace. The same with buying things; they disregard the seller and concentrate upon the wares they are buying, not thinking about whether their neighbor earns anything in the process; yet when they have something to sell they place the price so high, and hardly know how to stop praising their wares. This is true greed, self-love, and unrighteousness. So also the laborer often desires big wages while doing little work, or only half the work expected for it. This all comes from an impure heart which has no compassion for the neighbor.[28]

Andreas Ehrenpreis, one of the last significant leaders of the Hutterian Brethren in Moravia, writing in 1650, emphasized the economic dimensions of a common life characterized by justice and peace.

> Whoever claims to belong to Christ in love, but cannot give their possessions to the community for the sake of Christ and the poor, cannot deny that they love worldly goods, over which they have only been placed as caretakers for a time. Therefore Christ says, blessed are the poor in spirit, for theirs is the kingdom of heaven (Matt. 5:3). Yet Christ does not ask this simply for the sake of the poor, but also that his followers may be free and surrendered [*gelassen,* "yielded, at peace"] and not have a treasure on earth to which they tie their heart. . . . Let everyone seek the welfare of others.[29]

A Spirituality of Missional Vocation

Within sixteenth-century European Christendom there was very little sense of missional vocation – for a very simple reason. With the exception of a few Muslims and a Jewish minority the entire population of Europe had already been "christened" through infant baptism.

With the "discovery" of the New World, new missionary orders emerged within European Catholicism. While the Franciscans and the Dominicans were "christianizing" the pagan peoples of the Western Hemisphere, the armed forces of the Catholic, Lutheran, and Reformed countries of Europe were waging war against each other to determine which of the three groups would become the established church. What resulted was a political, rather than a religious, solution. Under the principle of *cuius regio, eius religio* ("whose realm, his religion") the religious affiliation of the ruler would automatically become that of the people. It was not until the Pietist revival at the end of the seventeenth century that a new sense of missional vocation emerged among classical Protestants. Even then, interest in mission arose primarily among the Pietists, on the margins of Christendom, outside the official church structures.

By contrast, the Anabaptist movement understood its vocation in missional terms already in the sixteenth century. Indeed, the Great Commission was one of their favorite texts. In their vision of the church, they considered themselves to be living in the era in which "the Lord's house shall be established as the highest of the mountains," when the nations of the earth will learn to walk in the ways of the Lord and God's law will go out through all the earth (Mic. 4:1–4).[30] Another favorite Anabaptist missionary texts was Psalm 24:1: "The earth is the Lord's and all that is in it, the world, and those who live in it." With this confident claim they felt authorized to evangelize anywhere and everywhere, even though it was forbidden by the established church and secular authorities.

Anabaptists in the sixteenth century were therefore forced to pursue their evangelizing mission outside existing legal structures. Remarkably, however, they not only survived as a hidden church, they also successfully evangelized under extremely adverse conditions. Work places soon became favorite locations for evangelical activity. And even in very difficult situations and within a highly patriarchal world, it was women who often became the most effective evangelizers – indeed, fully one-third of the early Anabaptist martyrs were women.

Thus, without recourse to socio-political, economic, or religious power – and without access to public means of communication such as official edicts and laws, the printing press, or higher education – the Anabaptists evangelized from the margins, witnessing to their faith "from below" by means of personal conversation, backed by the integrity of their life (and death!). In this process they subverted, in the name of God's reign of justice, the oppressive kingdoms of their time.

To conclude, the spirituality of the sixteenth-century Anabaptists, like that of the Christians of the first century, was characterized by the following elements:

1. it was inspired by the Spirit of the Living Christ;

2. it was oriented by the Scriptures, read and interpreted in the faith community;

3. it was consciously corporate – nourished and shared in the context of the community;

4. it was a Christ-centered spirituality of discipleship in which following Jesus was neither the privilege of an unusually committed minority, nor reserved for a "spiritual" elite, but the calling of the entire community of Christ;

5. it was characterized by a commitment to justice and peace in every aspect of life, as expressed by the biblical term "shalom"; and

6. it expressed itself by participating fully in God's saving mission in the world, a mission that anticipated, announced, and embodied the reign of God in this world.

Study Questions for Chapter 4

1. What about the Anabaptist understanding of Jesus was radically different from that of most Catholics and Protestants in the sixteenth century? How did their view of Jesus affect their daily lives?

2. How did the theology of two kingdoms – as the Anabaptists expressed it – affect their attitude towards the world? How did it shape their relationship to the state and their nonviolent stance?

3. The Anabaptists had very specific beliefs about nonviolence, coupled with beliefs about the role of the state in the world, and what their attitude should be towards the government. What were some of the most important of these beliefs?

4. How was this theology of nonviolence tested? How did the Anabaptist movement as a whole emerge from different tests? What were some reactions from specific Anabaptist thinkers to these different occasions that tested their nonviolence?

5. How did mission emerge as an important part of Christian faith across denominations? In what ways did Anabaptist mission differ from mission in the Catholic Church? What made Anabaptist mission so vital?

5

Spiritualities in Dialogue in the Twenty-First Century

John Howard Yoder, a well-known Mennonite theologian, has observed that radical reform movements tend to take on the mirror image of the very deficiencies that they have identified as in need of reform in the established churches.

For example, in a context where the church defined itself as a "sacramental communion," the radicals tended to eliminate the sacramental dimension from their ecclesiology in the hopes of recovering a dynamic vision and practice more relevant to their historical setting. Thus, in their reaction against an "idolatrous" liturgy, sixteenth-century Anabaptist worship deprived itself of some of the rich symbolism through which God's grace and love are communicated.[31]

However, in this desire to respond more faithfully to the gospel, the Anabaptists have not been the only ones in the history of the church whose spirituality has been impoverished. Roland Bainton, a renowned twentieth-century church historian, once suggested that Martin Luther's greatest tragedy consisted in not having Anabaptists nearby with whom to engage in meaningful dialogue. At the same time, in their reaction against

Luther's resolute emphasis on "justification by faith alone, without works" – and the almost inevitable lowering of ethical standards such an emphasis entailed – some Anabaptist groups emphasized obedience to the teachings of Christ so strongly, indeed almost exclusively, that they sometimes became victims of a sort of moral paralysis or legalism. This tension has lasted for many generations among some Anabaptist congregations.

In the introduction and conclusion to his book *From Anabaptist Seed,* the Canadian Mennonite historian Arnold Snyder offers an image that is both simple and profound in its reflection on the necessity for every spirituality to be accompanied by a particular identity.

All farmers know that in order to grow healthy plants that bear fruit, three things are necessary: good seed, good soil, and careful cultivation. The choice of the seed is crucial. Anyone who plants a mango seed and hopes to harvest oranges will be very disappointed. No amount of fertilizer will change the nature of the plant, contained as it was in the seed. But choosing and planting the right seed is not sufficient. The seed must be planted in fertile ground, or it withers and dies; and the young plants must be nourished and cared for, if one expects to harvest fruit.

Think of our churches as plants. Our church family first saw the light in the sixteenth century. It sprang from an Anabaptist seed. That original seed found fertile soil, was cultivated and nurtured, and produced an abundant harvest. The seeds of that harvest have been transplanted throughout the world now for almost 500 years. The basic nature of the seed is still visible in the plant, although cultivation and different climates have also changed the plant in important ways.

At the same time, however, Snyder also encourages us to continually take up the task of entering anew into fellowship and dialogue with Christians of other traditions regarding our respective spiritualities.

> There is much that we can and should learn from the testimony of these faithful witnesses. Nevertheless, one seed alone cannot be expected to fill God's entire vineyard. One variety of grape cannot provide every kind of wine, from sweet to dry, red to white.[32]

In the sixteenth century, Christians generally held the conviction that there was only one truth, and that this, of necessity, was to be found in only one tradition. For that reason, the established churches – who believed that they were the custodians of this truth – persecuted and even executed those in the reform movements who dared to question their authority. Yet ironic as it may seem, once they had consolidated their existence and established their identity, these same reform movements tended to assume a similar attitude toward their adversaries.

Thanks, in part at least, to the contributions of some of these radical reform movements – who assumed that God would continue to reveal his will and that we might continue to discover new truths from his holy Word – we are learning to appreciate the wide variety of gifts and legacies that have been preserved by each of the Christian traditions. As heirs of the Anabaptist tradition we also have valuable elements to contribute to this dialogue, even as we continue to learn from others.

In the remainder of this chapter we will seek to summarize some of the essential dimensions of Anabaptist spirituality as described in Chapters 3 and 4. Then, in light of the experiences that Anabaptists and other traditions have shared from the sixteenth century to the present, we suggest the following ways in which we can be mutually enriched as we enter into dialogue with other Christians and their distinctive spiritualities.

1. *Theology of the Spirit* In the context of established forms of Christendom in the sixteenth century, both Catholic and Protestant, the Anabaptist recovery of the Holy Spirit in their personal and community life proved to be life-giving. Their experience of three baptisms – of the Spirit, of water, and of blood – symbolized the depth and intensity of their encounter with God and with their neighbor. This was not only true in the sixteenth century, but throughout their history as they participated in God's mission in the world.

Some contemporary Anabaptists, however, have needed to experience this reality anew, through the gifts we have received from other traditions and other spiritualities. For example, thanks especially to the contributions of Pentecostal and charismatic Christians some of us have remembered and experienced afresh aspects of our spiritual tradition that had gone forgotten in our practice.

2. *Biblical Authority and Interpretation* In the context of Christendom, where the established tradition recognized the absolute authority of the church's hierarchy in matters of moral discernment and biblical interpretation, sixteenth-century Anabaptists' practice of the "hermeneutic community" – believers interpreting Scripture together in light of the Spirit – was virtually unique.

It was largely the Catholic Church's controversies with dissidents during their history that led to the almost absolute authority of the church's teaching office, or magisterium. Among Catholics this function was exercised by the priests and, in the last resort, by the bishop of Rome – the pope. Among Lutherans and other Protestants, the professors of theology in their universities and the clergy exercised this function, with the understanding that ultimately the prince was the highest bishop *(summus episcopus)* of the church in each territory.

For their part, the early Anabaptists felt that the will of God could be discerned and the Scriptures interpreted: 1) within the community of disciples committed to knowing and following God's will in their life and mission; 2) in their study of Scripture through which God continued to reveal himself; 3) as they gathered together under the inspiration and direction of the Holy Spirit present in their midst; and 4) in their commitment to put God's will for them into practice.

3. *Vision of the Church* In a context where the marks of the true church were understood largely in static or abstract categories – such as a "sacramental communion" (Catholic), a custodian of sound doctrine and worship practices (Reformed), or "where the Word is preached in truth and the sacraments are celebrated correctly" (Luther) – the Anabaptist vision of the church was outrageously bold. The Anabaptists viewed the church as the community of brothers and sisters authorized to interpret Scripture in order to practice the "rule of Christ," that is, to communicate God's forgiveness by restoring the errant brother or sister. In fact, Hubmaier and Grebel both regarded a commitment to practice and this new understanding of the church as an essential requirement for the baptism of new believers.

4. *Christ and Salvation* For the Anabaptists, salvation did not depend exclusively on the inner faith of the believer. Key phrases in the Schleitheim Confession include "the obedience of faith" and a call "to walk in the resurrection of Jesus Christ."[33] According to this vision, salvation is essentially relational and therefore inseparable from the

church. Salvation implies radical communion with both
God and neighbor and is incarnated in a Christ-like life in
the community of faith. The salvation theology of Michael
Sattler, for example, synthesizes both Catholic and classical Protestant elements. In reality, however, this vision
of salvation in the context of community was neither
Catholic nor Protestant, but distinctly Anabaptist. Salvation is personal, but it is not fundamentally individualistic
in the sense of a person being able to experience it inde-
pendently of a community of faith. Reconciliation with
God is always accompanied by reconciliation with the
neighbor. To follow Jesus is to truly know him. The Anabaptist concepts and practices of discipleship were derived
from their understanding of Jesus. They confessed Jesus as
"Lord to be followed" in all dimensions of their daily life.

5. *Justice and Peace* Since the fourth century – when the
Roman emperor Constantine brought about the close
relationship between the state and the church that has
come to characterize later Christian history and the corre-
sponding emergence of Augustine's defense of Christian
participation in warfare (the so-called just war) – the peace
witness of the church has been divided. We have not been
able to witness to the world with one voice on matters of
justice and peace. Instead, established Christianity has
sought to clarify when and under what circumstances
Christians might be able to participate in warfare without
sinning, thereby limiting, in theory at least, violence

among Christians but nonetheless justifying the practice of lethal violence.

However, this was not always the case for Christians. Among the earliest church fathers whose writings have been preserved, none justified the participation of Christians in warfare. The great majority of Christians in the pre-Constantinian church, as well as many of the radical reform movements within the church from Constantine to our own times, proclaimed with words and deeds their opposition to all forms of Christian violence.

On questions of war and peace, the mainstream churches – Orthodox, Catholic, and Protestant alike – have generally recognized their indebtedness to the radical reform movements and have come to expect from Anabaptists a witness and practice that promote relationships of justice and peace. In these times of "wars and rumors of wars" it is crucial that we nourish and retain this vision among our spiritual family of brothers and sisters. For example, before the US and British invasion of Iraq in 2003 it became clear that Anabaptists in the United States who have traditionally been absolute pacifists were no longer of one accord on matters of peace and war. In the events since the Gulf War the erosion of the peace conviction has continued among Anabaptists. Clearly, ongoing dialogue is needed not only at an interdenominational level, but also within our own denominations and congregations.

In my travels throughout the Mennonite world I have observed that it is possible to maintain an *ideology* of peace, apart from any accompanying concrete practices of these ideas. But it is virtually impossible to sustain an authentic *theology* of peace in the absence of concrete practices of justice and peace. Here we note the stark difference between ideology and theology as guiding principles for our lives. Authentic theology expresses truths that are lived out in practice, so that we may understand and live them more faithfully and communicate them more clearly in our missional witness.

Many of our brothers and sisters in the global south have reminded us of the essential relationship between justice and peace in our call to participate in God's shalom in the world. Menno Simons seems to have understood this clearly. Like the prophets of old, he understood justice in its biblical sense – as God giving us what we *need,* rather than what we *deserve.*

> All those who are born of God ... are ... to love their neighbors, not only with money and goods, but also after the example of their Lord and head, Jesus Christ, in an evangelical manner, with life and blood. They show mercy and love. ... No one among them is allowed to beg. ... They entertain those in distress. They take the stranger into their houses. They comfort the afflicted; assist the needy; clothe the naked; feed the hungry; do not turn their face from the poor; do not despise their own flesh.[34]

6. *Missionary Vocation* Undoubtedly, one of the most original contributions of the sixteenth-century Anabaptists to the wider church was their understanding that baptism was a commissioning to participate in God's mission in the world. In contrast to the Catholic missionary orders, where the missional commission was limited to those who had formally received the "orders" (or ordination) of the church, the Anabaptists were the first church community since the time of Constantine to apply the Great Commission to all of their members on the basis of their baptismal vows. In this commitment they restored the missionary vision and practice of the first-century church.

During the course of the twentieth century, Anabaptists in the United States recovered some of the missionary vision they had lost since the sixteenth century, not so much by reclaiming their radical historical roots, but more because of the influence of other traditions and Christian spiritualities which gave rise to the Protestant mission movement. It has taken many years for this missionary vision to root itself deeply through a fresh reading of Scriptures and a rediscovery of our own radical history.

Another challenge for the descendants of the early Anabaptists is to recover the full dimensions of justice and peace in our evangelization. Here our tendency to listen more to the voices around us than to embrace a radical reading of Scriptures has led us to regard justice and peace more as a matter of Christian ethics than as qualities at the very heart of the New Testament gospel. Yet in the New Testament, the gospel is a gospel of peace!

In order to communicate the gospel authentically, Christians must love their enemies, just as God loves his enemies. "While we still were sinners," we read in Romans, "Christ died for us" (Rom. 5:8). Here we find ourselves face-to-face with the scandal of Jesus' messianic mission. Christ came proclaiming the gospel of peace to the outsiders, the disinherited, the marginalized – to all who were thought to be the adversaries of God.

We who are the heirs of the sixteenth-century Anabaptists still have much to learn from our brothers and sisters in other Christian traditions. In our life together with brothers and sisters in the greater family of faith we do not enjoy the luxury of being able to choose our spiritual ancestors. We are all heirs of one tradition or another. The life and mission of the universal church will be greatly blessed when all of these traditions bring their contributions to the table of fraternal communion.

Many years ago René Padilla, a highly-respected Latin American theologian and biblical scholar, shared with me his conviction that our theological understanding will finally be complete only when all traditions within the Christian church have been able to bring to the table their experiences of God's grace and of God's project to restore both humanity and creation.

In the light of the enormity of the promise and challenge before us the urgent questions we face will include the following: 1) What contributions do we need to receive from our brothers and sisters in other traditions as they seek to live out God's purposes in their midst? 2) What contributions do our brothers and sisters in other traditions hope to receive from us in our attempts to be faithful to God's call in our lives? 3) How can we all participate more faithfully in God's saving purposes, as co-participants in God's mission in the world?

Study Questions for Chapter 5

1. In the beginning of this section, the author describes
    how religious reform movements often experience the
    same problems or deficiencies that were in the churches
    that they originally left or split from in the process of
    reformation. How was this true for the Anabaptists
    historically? How is it true today? How might inter-
    denominational dialogue help address this problem?

2. What is so important about believing that God will
    continually reveal his truth to his followers? How did
    this attitude of continual discovery and renewal affect
    Anabaptists through history? What should our attitude
    as Anabaptists in the twenty-first century be? Do you
    experience God's Word as already fully developed or in
    the process of unfolding?

3. What about the Holy Spirit has been most important
    throughout the history of Anabaptism? How have con-
    temporary Anabaptists reawakened to the vitality and
    power of the Holy Spirit? What role have other denomi-
    nations played?

4. According to the author, the Anabaptist understanding
    of the church was considered very bold and different
    in its historical context. What vision did Anabaptist
    thinkers hold of the church? In what ways did their
    concept of church differ from that of other Christians?

5. What is the Anabaptist understanding of salvation? How does it relate to community? Why is salvation something to be shared, or something that happens with fellow believers?

6. How have other denominations viewed the Anabaptist peace stance? Where does this peace stance come from? In what ways can contemporary Anabaptists renew their commitment to peace?

7. How has Anabaptist mission differed from that of other churches? What effect has this had throughout history? In what ways have contemporary Anabaptists recovered their missionary zeal? How can twenty-first-century Anabaptists keep their commitment to mission?

Conclusion: Radical Spirituality

In the light of the great variety of Christian spiritualities circulating today, some of which are inadequate or even deformed, it is absolutely necessary that we return to our roots in Jesus and to the community inspired by his Spirit in the first century in order to re-orient our own spirituality.

In marked contrast to many traditional spiritualities, the Bible does not allow the distinctions we often make between the inner and the outer, or between the spiritual and the material, or between believing and doing. For many, Mother Teresa's community in Calcutta is an example of an authentic Christian spirituality. For Mother Teresa, to touch the untouchables was to touch the body of Christ. To love in an utterly unselfish way was, for her, a form of prayer. She did not stop praying to serve, nor did she stop serving to pray. Authentic spirituality is all-embracing.

The cross of Jesus is the clearest model of a spirituality that is authentically Christian. It is at once a sign of absolute identification with God and an expression of God's solidarity with humanity. In the cross, the spirit of Jesus is reflected most clearly. This is the spirituality that his disciples are called to practice. The cross is simultaneously the most eloquent prayer of intercession to the Father on behalf of humanity, and the clearest and the most powerful response of God to the powers of evil. In the cross of Jesus, and in the cross borne by his followers, we find the very essence of Christian spirituality.

A truly authentic Christian spirituality, therefore, will not be shapeless. It will take forms that are truly visible and salvific. Christian spirituality is the process of following Jesus Christ under the inspiration of the Spirit in the context of a shared life within the messianic community. For this reason, Christian spirituality is Trinitarian: it is lived in absolute dependence on God the Father, oriented toward the model of Jesus, and empowered by the impulse and inspiration of the Holy Spirit.

A fully Christian spirituality – like that which we see reflected in the messianic community of the first century – is above all rooted in God's grace and expressed concretely in following Jesus. This means that our entire life is lived in the power of the Spirit of Jesus Christ himself. An authentic Christian spirituality will be nourished and shared in the context of the community of the living Christ. From the biblical perspective the idea of a "solitary saint" is an impossibility.

Finally, a fully Christian spirituality will be incarnated in mission – God's mission in the world carried out with unique clarity and power by Jesus of Nazareth, as he lived under the impulse and inspiration of God's Spirit.

For those of us who share the radical Anabaptist tradition, it is especially interesting to note the points of overlap between the sixteenth-century Anabaptists and the spirituality of the early Christian community in the first century. The same could be said of the heirs of other Christian traditions, equally radical in their spirituality rooted in Jesus Christ and in the first-century messianic community. The spirituality that characterized the Anabaptist movement depended on the powerful intervention of the Spirit of the risen Christ. But what distinguished the Anabaptists most from other traditions was undoubtedly their practices and understanding of the church – for them, participation in the Christian community was absolutely essential. The rich and varied dimensions of this participation were reflected in the four symbols of community that marked the Anabaptists' corporate spirituality.

In *baptism* the Anabaptists committed themselves to following Christ, to "walk in the resurrection," and to live in "the obedience of faith" as they themselves confessed. But they also saw themselves as fully commissioned to participate in God's mission in the world. And this, in marked contrast with other traditions, was the privilege of all Christians, not simply of the clergy. In baptism, Anabaptists also committed themselves to receive and to offer *counsel and discipline* according to "the rule of Christ" (Matt. 18:15–20), and they committed themselves to *mutual sharing* – helping one another with their material, as well as their spiritual, needs. In their celebration of the *Lord's Supper,* Anabaptists renewed their vows to follow Jesus, even to the point of laying down their lives for their fellow humans, just as Jesus had done.

They confessed that Jesus was not only to be revered as a savior or as the final judge, but also as the Lord to be followed in a life of daily discipleship. Their spirituality was marked by this vision. Their participation in the reign of God, in which Jesus was already Lord, led the Anabaptists to adopt a spirituality characterized by justice and peace, just as Jesus had proclaimed and practiced. All of this led the Anabaptists to embrace, to a remarkable degree for their time, a spirituality marked by the missional vocation implied in their understanding of baptism.

The spiritual heirs of the Radical Reformation of the sixteenth-century certainly have no monopoly on this kind of spirituality. All who are workers in the Lord's vineyard have contributions to make toward a recovery of the Christian spirituality reflected in the life of the early church. Neither orthodoxy nor heterodoxy is automatically passed on from one generation to another. Therefore every new generation has the opportunity and the responsibility to engage once again in mutual dialogue in their search for the new forms that an authentically Christian spirituality will take in their midst.

In the sense that Christian spirituality consists of following Jesus of Nazareth under the impulse of the

Spirit, there is only one spirituality. However, in the sense that Christians seek to follow Jesus, each in his or her own particular historical context, there can be a diversity of Christian spiritualities. These differences are found in the variety of historical, geographic, and cultural settings in which discipleship is practiced. All of our spiritualities, without exception, can be enriched – thanks be to God! – through the contributions of brothers and sisters in other traditions.

Undoubtedly, the essential elements of authentic spirituality that we have noted in Jesus and in the early church will be of lasting validity. Among other things they will include a vital role of the Spirit, a corporate communal church life that is truly transforming, an understanding of Christ and salvation that are truly salvific – that is, reconciling us with God and with our fellow humans, including our adversaries – and communal relationships marked by the justice and peace that characterize life under God's reign. This is the restored communion of the new creation that we proclaim in deed and word in the missional vocation that we share.

Study Questions for Chapter 6

1. According to the author, what are some of the most important aspects of authentic spirituality? What does life look like for someone (or a community) living a true Christian spirituality? How does mission relate to Christian spirituality?

2. How is Christian spirituality a process, and not a state of being? Why is this distinction key to every aspect of Anabaptist belief?

3. Why is dialogue so important in our attempt to live out authentic Christian spirituality? In what ways does dialogue bring renewal to a church that may think it has a "monopoly" on truth or authenticity?

4. What aspects of Anabaptist spirituality does the author considers most important? How do they complement one another?

Responses from the
Global Anabaptist Church

The Work of the Holy Spirit in the Mennonite Churches of the Democratic Republic of Congo

Mvwala C. Katshinga

According to Acts 2, the church originates from the Holy Spirit, and the Holy Spirit is the invisible God made visible in the actions of the men and women who have believed in Jesus Christ. Consequently, the Holy Spirit is God's power, which sets the believer in motion in word, spirit, and action in order to make God's love for creation a reality. This divine power is permanent and available everywhere, including the Democratic Republic of Congo (DR Congo), where it has produced tangible fruit in the Mennonite churches.

The manifestation of the Holy Spirit in the Mennonite churches in DR Congo can be seen during three distinct periods: the North American missionary activity, the establishment of local churches, and the missionary outreach and cross-cultural engagement of the local churches.

North American Mennonite Missionary Activity

We can never say it often enough: the Christian faith according to the Anabaptist interpretation came to DR Congo through the heartfelt obedience of North Ameri-

---

Mvwala C. Katshinga is a Mennonite missiologist, linguist, and translator, as well as a senior lecturer at the Université Pédagogique National, Kinshasa, DR Congo.

can Anabaptists to the Holy Spirit and to Jesus' words in Matthew 28:18–20.

Since the nineteenth century, two major impulses have pushed Western people to conquer the world in general and Africa in particular: human-centered desires (colonization, slavery, tourism, exploration, scientific research, etc.) and a Christ-centered desire to bring the good news of Jesus Christ in all its aspects to people who do not know about it.

Although the colonizers undertook enormous efforts to make a name for themselves and to achieve power and fortune, the missionaries, impassioned by the love of others that the Holy Spirit provides, did not make sacrifices for personal gain. They gave their lives so that others (we) would know eternal life in Jesus Christ. This is the example set by the crucified Christ, the missionary par excellence, who knew in advance what would happen to him.

As we can verify, only the Spirit of God can give someone such a strong conviction to go save those they do not know in an unknown place, making sacrifices to live in a context in which their life is neither certain nor secure, in order to rebuild a physical and spiritual world destroyed by sin.

Thus we can paraphrase 2 Peter 1:21 by saying that it is because they were moved by the Holy Spirit that North American Anabaptists spread out in Africa in general and in DR Congo in particular, proof of their obedience to the Great Commission.

But how did the Holy Spirit water and bring to fruit this seed planted by the Mennonite mission in the Belgian Congo? The process of establishing local churches is a good testimony to the active power of the Holy Spirit.

Establishment of Local Mennonite Churches

Mennonite missionary activity was launched in the Congo in the early twentieth century by the Congo Inland Mission (CIM) with the help of Africa Inter-Mennonite Mission (AIMM). Through the work of missionary Lawrence B. Haigh, CIM began to evangelize Congolese people in 1911 in the Western Kasai province, at Kalamba and at Ndjoko-Punda, not far from Tshikapa.

The churches planted by CIM grew to become the current Mennonite Church of Congo (CMCo). Later, in the 1980s, the Evangelical Mennonite Church grew out of CMCo following separatist conflicts between eastern and western groups in Kasai.

In addition, in 1920, the Mennonite Brethren also started a new missionary field, thanks to Aaron and Ernestina Janzen, a former CIM missionary couple. The Janzens first established a mission station at Kikandji, which was transferred two years later to Kafumba.

With support from the American Mennonite Brethren Mission, this mission work extended into the Kwilu region and soon after into the Kwango area. These churches became what is now called the Mennonite Brethren

Church of Congo (CEFMC), having registered as a denomination in 1945.

Today the three Mennonite church groupings in DR Congo – the Mennonite Church of Congo, the Mennonite Brethren Church of Congo, and the Evangelical Mennonite Church of Congo – have a total of nearly 250,000 members, with churches in ten of the eleven provinces of the country.

The development, expansion, and establishment of the Christian faith according to Anabaptist biblical understanding has been accompanied by tangible expressions of God's Spirit, including many people converted to the Good News, deliverance from illiteracy and lack of education, the emergence of priestly vocations for men and women, intertribal discipleship, and missionary engagement with individuals and churches.

Missionary and Cross-Cultural Outreach of Local Churches
After the phase of internal growth and development, the Mennonite churches in DR Congo, moved by the Holy Spirit, spontaneously began to undertake cross-cultural evangelization, first in Kinshasa among Muslim people, diplomats, and refugees, then in the different border areas of the country with people from the nine neighboring countries.

Thanks again to the Holy Spirit, Mennonite churches planted local churches in Angola (where many members are Mennonites who were formerly from DR Congo) and in Congo-Brazzaville. And the vision to reach Rwanda and Burundi from churches planted along the African Great Lakes, notably from Bukavu and Uvira, is being realized.

Finally, there has been missionary activity among the Pygmy people (the Batwa) of the Congolese equatorial forest since 1998, with four ordained Batwa pastors actively working there. The significant Congolese Mennonite diaspora is also mobilizing for evangelization in their host countries and planting local churches. In Durban, South Africa, for example, a Mennonite church is functioning and local vocations are being reported. We can thus confirm that the Holy Spirit is indeed at work in the church of DR Congo.

Reflections on Driver's Life Together in the Spirit

I believe that this book provides a very rich and necessary doctrinal manual for the training of Anabaptist church members throughout the world. This book offers theological and historical information that is necessary for all generations. It is a precious instrument for the rediscovery of the Anabaptist identity and of doctrinal reorientation. I strongly suggest that it be translated into different languages and made accessible to members of Anabaptist churches and to their religious partners through interdenominational dialogue. Some sections of the book, however, could be improved, as suggested below.

In my opinion, Driver has not reviewed all aspects of the question of discipline. I sense that his perspective is very "democratized." To speak of discipline in the church, one must always be aware of the indiscipline which is lying in wait, and which characterizes human beings in general and Christians, even Anabaptists, in particular. The church of our times must not see the love of God as blessing misbehavior. The witness of a disciplined church and disciplined Christians has a significant influence on non-Christians. To be in the world without being of the world (John 17:14–17) requires personal and collective discipline in all areas of life.

Thus, it is very significant that the first Anabaptists inscribed discipline as one of the fundamental elements of faith in the Schleitheim Confession (1527). It is thanks to their individual and collective discipline that some of the first Anabaptists were willing to lose their nationality, and to even to die, in order to preserve the role and the life of the church in the face of the political and cultural intrusions of their times.

Certainly, whether it is punitive or not, discipline in the church is intended to restore the person involved (1 Cor. 5:1–5; Prov. 19:18). In other words, the ultimate objective of the disciplinary process outlined in three steps in Matthew 18:15–18 is to put the brother or the sister who has sinned on the path to repentance.

But legalists favor the punitive aspects of the disciplinary procedure ("but if the offender refuses to listen even to the church, let him be to you as a Gentile and a tax collector," which is actually step 3 and forget the persuasive and training aspects of step 1 ("go and point out the fault when the two of you are alone") and step 2 ("if you are not listened to, take one or two others along with you"). On the other hand, it is liberal and dangerous for the church to bypass punitive discipline for a favored person who refuses to listen to his brother or sister in Christ and to his church.

In short, it would be better if Driver would clearly explain the biblical application of this essential aspect of our doctrine with a strong focus on discipline "in an Anabaptist way" – its mode of administration, its levels of application, and its objectives. Otherwise, churches risk becoming centers for the democratization of homosexuality, sorcery, clericalism, and other problems which our sixteenth-century predecessors criticized with good reason.

It is thus a moral task, even a commandment of faith, that, through the Mennonite World Conference, we regularly and solemnly give our interpretation of the evils that are eroding our local churches.

Hopes for the Future of the MWC Churches

In regards to interdenominational dialogue, we must proceed with caution. MWC must open itself up very carefully to others. But is this an interreligious dialogue? For what purpose? How far can we go and with whom can we

dialogue? All dialogue is a negotiation and every negotiation sometimes requires that each party involved give
up some of its beginning arguments; that is, it must make
concessions. How will others challenge us and what are
we ready to concede doctrinally? Must we dialogue, for
example, with denominations that preach that salvation
can be found in all religions? (Acts 4:12)

MWC must also encourage member churches to "liber-
ate" the ministry of women (Gal. 3:25–28). I call on MWC
to initiate a World Summit of Anabaptist Women like that
of the Youth. God does not give us the gifts of the Holy
Spirit based on whether we are men or women. The ordination of women pastors must no longer be a question
which is taboo.

Reflection on Driver's *Life Together in the Spirit* from an Indian Point of View

Christina Asheervadam

John Driver's book, *Life Together in the Spirit,* could be very helpful to the Indian church. Spirituality has become popular among other faiths and groups in India – "Hindu spirituality," "Dalit spirituality," "feminist spirituality," "ecumenical spirituality," etc. Driver, in turn, emphasizes that the power of the Holy Spirit leads us into spirituality, noting that "a truly evangelical spirituality implies solidarity with the suffering, death, and resurrection of Jesus."

The biblical understanding of spirituality is living life according to the direction and guidance of the Holy Spirit. The Holy Spirit is available for everyone (Acts 2:16–21). He gives us wisdom in making right decisions (Jerusalem Council in Acts 15). He controls everything (Eph. 5:18). He guides the messengers (Phillip in Acts 8:29; Paul and John in Acts 8:14). He designates believers to carry out his mission (Barnabas and Paul, Acts 13:2), guides people from place to place (Acts 16:6–10), and foretells the future, such as the famine in the days of Claudius and Paul's arrest in Jerusalem (Acts 11:28; 21:11). The Holy Spirit gives us power to live a Christian life (Rom. 8:2), unites

Christina Asheervadam is Director of the Center for Peace and Conflict Resolution Studies at Mennonite Brethren Centenary Bible College in Hyderabad, Andhra Pradesh, India.

believers (Eph. 4:3), empowers, motivates, energizes, supports (1 Chron. 12:18), counsels, and enables us to reach out to the whole world. Believers can claim the power of the Holy Spirit to do Christ's work and establish shalom on the earth. The Holy Spirit thus gives strength to do extraordinary tasks (Judg. 3:10–11).

The Holy Spirit is God's gift to humankind, dwelling with us until the end of the world as Jesus promised. The Holy Spirit descended to live among us and enable us to live a spiritual life. Driver insists that this spirituality has to be reflected in our day-to-day life. The following saying captures this idea well: "The stream of the Holy Spirit is the native element for a Christian, as much as water is the natural element for a fish." Hence, Christian spirituality involves both word and deed.

The Indian Context

India has a unique multi-religious and multicultural society. Within this context the Hindu-patronized caste system recognizes four major groups: Brahmins (priests), Kshatriyas (kings and soldiers), Vyshyas (business people), and Sudras (people who do menial jobs). Those who are born outside this caste system are called Panchamas or Dalits. Caste is assigned by birth and cannot be changed through religious conversion or accumulation of wealth.

Within the caste system, the Dalits (along with other groups such as the Tribals) are dehumanized. They are downtrodden, marginalized, and treated as untouchables. They are exploited, oppressed, and suppressed, often denied education, employment, and basic human rights and privileges. Women are raped and children exploited as bonded laborers by the high caste people. Most importantly, the government has not protected their rights. Even today, when Dalits convert to Christianity, they lose government jobs and privileges.

Hindus are the religious majority in India. They worship many gods and goddesses – they believe there are as many as 330 million. The Dalits and Tribals have their own gods and goddesses, and all of them believe in spirits. They believe that there are good spirits that guide them and rescue them in their problems and difficulties. Especially in rural areas, people also believe that evil spirits exist who will attack and harm them. This leads to a belief in witchcraft and in the goddess *Kali* who will rescue them from evil spirits. They believe that when a devotee is filled with the spirit of *Kali* he or she will have the power to cast out the demonic spirit from the possessed person. The Christian gospel reached into this context in India.

Spirituality in the Mennonite Church

Missionaries in India attempted to improve the lives of Dalits and Tribals socially, politically, economically, and religiously. To that end, missionaries focused not only on evangelism but also on education, medicine, and philanthropy. They built schools, hospitals, and churches for the holistic transformation of these afflicted people. Throughout the Indian church today the highest percentage of believers are from Dalit, Tribal, and Adivasi communities – indeed, in the Mennonite Brethren Church some 90 percent of believers are drawn from these backgrounds.

The Mennonite Brethren missionaries came to India with a powerful message and taught about the power of the Holy Spirit against evil spirits and witchcraft. Some of the grandchildren of the early converts who worked as preachers, especially in the villages, remember their grandparents saying that without the power of the Holy Spirit, it would not have been possible for them to work against evil spirits, witchcraft, and the dominant power of caste and creeds in the society. Their dependence on the Holy Spirit was very strong, and it continues even today in our churches. As Rev. Dr. P. B. Arnold, the president of the church's governing council, recently remarked, "Today the Holy Spirit is effectively working in our Mennonite Brethren Church."

Historically, Indian Mennonite Brethren have come from the poorest-of-poor backgrounds. The church was established in Andhra Pradesh, in the drought-prone Mahabubnagar district in current-day Telengana. But whereas the people were once economically very poor, now, by God's grace, their lives have been changed and, as the Spirit enables them, they have become generous givers to their local churches. They are contributing to build huge church buildings and spread the gospel.

As the Holy Spirit guides and enables the churches, many local churches are taking initiative and traveling to the villages, sharing the gospel during weekends and holidays, especially in summer vacation. Many times they have been attacked by Hindu militant groups. Yet the church, rooted in the Word of God and dependent on the Holy Spirit for guidance and strength, continues to participate in this ministry. In some villages several of our pastors were denied housing; but they did not give up and instead patiently waited for doors to open. Today there is a strong presence of the church in these villages.

Anti-Christian persecution and the Anti-Conversion Bill are major challenges for the church at this time. In many states of India recently, atrocities focused on Christians have become common. Churches have been destroyed and burnt in Delhi, Odyssa, and Bengaluru. Pastors have been killed, nuns raped, and believers threatened by Hindu militant groups. Recently in Uttar Pradesh, Hindu militant groups forcefully re-converted some of the Christians to the Hindu religion in the name of *Ghar Vapasi,* which means "homecoming." This is a burning issue right now. One church leader said in a television news interview, "Father, forgive them, for they do not know what they are doing." Another church leader said that "this is an opportunity to show our tolerance towards them."

This is nothing but spirituality. Engaging and participating in the restoration process presents inescapable demands on Christians to engage in costly acts of forgiveness, reconciliation, justice, and peace building; this is Christian spirituality.

Though the church often finds itself facing unfavorable situations, the Holy Spirit enables the local churches to endure any situation. "The cross of Jesus offers us the clearest model of an authentically Christian spirituality, reflected in the teachings of the New Testament," writes Driver. Although the cross was once used as a symbol of the curse, Jesus redefined the cross as a symbol of love, forgiveness, endurance, patience, reconciliation, acceptance, availability, sacrifice, and suffering. Hence, "take up the cross and follow me" means reflecting spirituality every day in and through our life.

Apart from persecution, the church faces additional challenges, including hunger, poverty, unemployment, forced migration, discrimination, injustice, and death. Dalit Christians are denied job opportunities and privileges from the government. Discrimination against women is another significant concern. In India, women have been treated as second-class citizens both outside and within the church. Until recently, they were denied education and employment. In some of the churches, their services went unrecognized even though they were actively involved. Now in the Mennonite Brethren Church, however, women are ordained and have formed Women Fellowships. As a result we have a strong All-India Mennonite Women

Conference with around sixty to seventy ordained women. Mennonite Brethren conference leadership also requires that every local church administration should have one woman representative.

In the midst of all these adverse situations, we can still experience the presence of Holy Spirit in worship, singing, and fellowship. Thanks to this Spirit, today we have more than a thousand congregations and over two hundred thousand baptized members in India.

We can see how the first-century disciples, filled with the Holy Spirit, reflected this spirituality in every aspect of life. They were encouraged in their disappointments, guided when they were confused, and empowered to face challenges. They received discernment in resolving major issues. They led others into faith, performed miracles, and lived as witnesses of Christ.

We need to remember that the Holy Spirit is a permanent gift to the church until our Savior returns. It is not a gift to just one generation or people, but the gift and promise of God to all people in all places. Yet having a gift does not in itself signify spiritual authority or maturity. The gift is given for service, not as a symbol of spiritual status. There should be no room in the church for fights over status. Indeed, spirituality can be seen in actions and not in mere words. When a church doesn't reflect what God intended, then it is a dead church. The Spirit-filled church is known by its actions rather than for speaking in strange tongues.

Today we do not see much emphasis on the work of the Holy Spirit in some of the major church traditions. But we as Anabaptists need to constantly renew our spirituality so that we will be strengthened and capable of facing severe persecutions. We are glad that we are part of this historic Anabaptist family. Once again, we are reminded through John Driver's book that we need to revive our spirituality, remain rooted in the Spirit of Jesus Christ, and maintain our distinct witness within Christianity in practices and life.

Alternative Communities as Accents of the Spirit

Rafael Zaracho

Driver's notion of spirituality – marked by a life of action and full of participation in the social order – offers us a great opportunity to reflect on, repent of, and correct the course and form of our communal life in a region with "open veins" (in Eduardo Galeano's words) of inequality and social need. In addition, as we reflect on the life of our "fellowship of love" we must remember our Anabaptist historical and theological tendency toward sectarianism and remain attentive to the ways in which this inclination has been expressed in our particular regions.

There is an increasing need, at least in Latin America, to be led by the Spirit in forming alternative communities where we come together to celebrate our differences and work for the extension of God's kingdom. We can appreciate the historical and theological differences expressed in our various fellowships as we come to see them as accents of the Spirit. These accents suggest the importance of our believing communities as places where we name, prioritize, celebrate, and conserve unique dimensions of our relationships with our God, our brothers and sisters, and our contexts.

Rafael Zaracho is a professor at Instituto Bíblico Asunción in Paraguay and secretary of the MWC Mission Commission.

Seeing our own cultural and theological inclinations, along with those of other traditions, as accents of the Spirit reframes Babel as an image of blessing. Babel becomes an image of blessing because it creates diversity and reveals any attempt at all-encompassing power as a "spell." The miracle of Pentecost, then, redeems Babel and opens the possibility of understanding each other through the fellowship of love that the Spirit creates. This fellowship enables moments and events in which we may see, feel, and taste the work of the Spirit in our personal and communal lives.

Seeing our differences as accents of the Spirit calls us to become discerning communities that question the course and consequences of our beliefs and practices. It invites us to value and judge the diversity of our fellowships by their life-giving quality and by their promotion of a reconciled creation.

As communities, we will work for the extension of God's kingdom when we perceive that our communal life, like that of other traditions, is part of God's work in the world.

First, the kingdom of God, or the idea of "God at work," nurtures both the mission and identity of these communities. God desires to form communities that begin to live as a "foretaste of the future." We become communities by the gift that comes and gathers us. The Spirit who promotes life, restoration, reconciliation, and resurrection gathers us as brothers and sisters. As communities our hope, prayer, and task is to engage in this ongoing process so that the Spirit may guide us to become fellowships of love.

Second, the idea of "God at work" sparks our hope and imagination. The restoration and resurrection we experience gives us hope for a new creation. This image of a new creation entices, frees, and catapults our imagination beyond the logic or reality of this world to see that a different world is possible, and it leads us to become alternative communities. This transformation is possible because our identity is built around this gift that comes and gathers us. As we become filled with the hope of a different reality, we may find companions who share our desires, preferences, and hopes. Our Anabaptist background offers us a rich tradition of both success and failure in being such communities.

As we seek to become alternative communities, we recognize the presence of the Spirit in us, in our midst, and in the world. We see the work of the Spirit enabling and promoting fellowship of love with others. As believing communities, we gather around a common table and enjoy the bread and wine. We see in the bread and wine symbols and expressions of grace, celebration, and hope. Our joy rests on the hope of the resurrection of the body. Our church communities, as the resurrected body of Christ (1 Cor. 12:12–27), proclaim the redemption of the body as expressed in concrete realities such as working conditions, salary, health, housing, and freedom from fear. Our communities become prophetic and poetic testimonies and symbols of solidarity, spaces where we hope, pray, and work at "extending the table."

Such communities become possible when their members are guided by the Spirit of the "broken bread" as they relate to each other in word and action. Their distinguishing mark is a loving compassion expressed in multiple mutual relationships. This is what Driver calls "radical spirituality." As believing communities, we are aware of our tendency to fall short in discerning God's presence in our experiences and in the world. At this point, it becomes crucial to see our historical-theological differences as accents of the Spirit because they will allow us to recognize how the Spirit has been working – and continues to work – in and through fellowships of love.

We pray, therefore, that our common desires and hopes may become flesh in and through fellowships of love that celebrate and foster life, reconciliation, restoration, and resurrection. As believing communities, as accents of the Spirit, our hopes become groans that are our prayers. We share this groan with the entire creation (Rom. 8: 19–27).

The Fruits of the Spirit

Hermann Woelke

It was both inspiring and renewing to read this book by John Driver, who has been my teacher on multiple occasions. I have learned much from him.

In the Latin American world, in which I live and work, the Holy Spirit is often associated with loud music and spontaneous and emotional expressions. In our congregation, however, we stress that faith in God is experienced especially through the voice of the Holy Spirit – the voice of God in our lives. That voice helps, guides, and teaches us in specific situations. It will always be heard within the framework of the teachings of the Bible and obedience to our Lord and Savior Jesus Christ, as we seek to be transformed in his image. Sometimes it will challenge us to re-read the Bible from a new perspective. We encourage our brothers and sisters to study the Bible and attend to what the Holy Spirit is saying to them through it.

Another important aspect of the Holy Spirit's activity is discernment (1 Cor. 2:14–15). Although the Holy Spirit also manifests itself through miracles, supernatural appearances, and emotions, these do not form the foundation for judgment in the Old Testament or the New. Jesus taught his disciples that we will be known and judged by

Hermann Woelke is coordinator of the Study Center of the Mennonite Churches of Uruguay.

our fruit (Matt. 7:16–20). The New Testament offers the following examples of fruit:

Luke 3:8 The "fruit of repentance," in other words, a changed life

Hebrews 13:15 The fruit of worship and witness

Philippians 1:11 The fruit of justice, that a person who follows Christ grows in understanding of justice and in just action

Romans 6:22 The fruit of holiness, of separation from evil and dedication to God

Galatians 5:22–23 The fruits of the Spirit – love, joy, peace, patience, kindness, goodness, faithfulness, gentleness, and self-control

Romans 15:26–28 Material aid as good fruit

Romans 16:5 People who have converted because of our testimony

These fruits – repentance, worship, justice, holiness, the fruits of the Spirit described in Galatians, material aid, and conversions – identify the one who possesses them as a child of God.

The Holy Spirit also makes itself known through signs and gifts that accompany those who believe (Mark 16:17) – supernatural ones as well as those that are more practical. All of these will produce good fruits for the common good (1 Cor. 12:7).

Driver's emphasis on a spirituality grounded in the cross, as explained at the beginning and developed throughout the book, revives this central theme – the spiritual practice of following Jesus in the path that he traveled through the cross to glory with his Father.

Driver affirms that baptism is not simply a symbol of the spirituality of the cross of Christ, but that the baptismal vows are also a commitment to participate in the mission of God in the world, something that is surely worth recovering in our baptismal vows. On the next page he writes:

> The life and mission of the universal church will be greatly blessed when all of these traditions bring their contributions to the table of fraternal communion. . . . In the light of the enormity of the promise and challenge before us the urgent questions we face will include the following: 1) What contributions do we need to receive from our brothers and sisters in other traditions as they seek to live out God's purposes in their midst? 2) What contributions do our brothers and sisters in other traditions hope to receive from us in our attempts to be faithful to God's call in our lives? 3) How can we all participate more faithfully in God's saving purposes, as co-participants in God's mission in the world?

I want to read this passage in the broader context of this book, given that the variety of Christian traditions is so vast and not always based in the Word of God. It would be dangerous to share traditions without keeping in mind the principles presented in the rest of the book. Biblical passages such as the following from Ephesians provide discernment, direction, and purpose for sharing among traditions:

> The gifts he gave were that some would be apostles, some prophets, some evangelists, some pastors and teachers, to equip the saints for the work of ministry, for building up the body of Christ, until all of us come to the unity of the faith and of the knowledge of the Son of God, to maturity, to the measure of the full stature of Christ. We must no longer be children, tossed to and fro and blown about by every wind of doctrine, by people's trickery, by their craftiness in deceitful scheming. But speaking the truth in love, we must grow up in every way into him who is the head, into Christ, from whom the whole body, joined and knit together by every ligament with which it is equipped, as each part is working properly, promotes the body's growth in building itself up in love. (Eph. 4:11–16)

Sharing among traditions will be enriching and promote growth as long as the spirituality of Jesus Christ, as presented in this book, is the standard for discernment as well as the path and ultimate goal in the search for growth. Driver points to this in one of the final paragraphs:

> In the sense that Christian spirituality consists of following Jesus of Nazareth under the impulse of the Spirit, there is only one spirituality. However, in the sense that Christians seek to follow Jesus, each in his or her own particular historical context, there can be a diversity of Christian spiritualities. These differences are found in the variety of historical, geographic, and cultural settings in which discipleship is practiced. All of our spiritualities, without exception, can be enriched – thanks be to God! – through the contributions of brothers and sisters in other traditions.

Therefore we should never forget that only in Jesus Christ will we be able to find the model of true Christian spirituality, even though it has diverse expressions in different historical, cultural, and geographic contexts.

We thank God for the way in which he shows himself in our lives through his Holy Spirit, bringing healing, restoration, and blessing. But above all, we thank God for giving us the power to be his witness (martyrs, Acts 1:8). We want to grow in our relationship with God. May we hear his Word through the Holy Spirit and be led to bear much good fruit, to use the gifts of the Spirit in service to God to serve others, and to have the strength to live sanctified lives accompanied by supernatural signs (Mark 16:15–18).

Disciples' Daily Life as Spiritual Formation: Toward a Paradigm Shift of Christian Spirituality

Chiou-Lang "Paulus" Pan

John Driver's book, *Life Together in the Spirit,* is a timely resource for Taiwanese Mennonites looking to draw on the theological resources of their Anabaptist roots. Pursuing spiritual growth in order to be a better Christian has been a major concern among the Chinese churches for decades, and as well as one of the most important ministries for pastors. Current spirituality in Chinese churches reflects the influences of both modern educational theory and the Confucian concept of the cultivation of perfect humanity toward absolute wisdom. Many Christians will most likely equate spiritual formation with personal practices like Bible reading, prayer, or fasting. Therefore, in addition to a series of disciple-making courses, personal Bible study (especially in the early morning) and prayer have become the common paradigm of spiritual growth for believers. Some churches took these two exercises as a standard measure of spiritual growth, illustrated in the Chinese saying, "Do not touch sacred work with profane hands." Here, "sacred hands" means praying hands. Later in our history, participating in church ministries and tithing

Chiou-Lang "Paulus" Pan is a professor at Central Taiwan College and Theological Seminary and a member of the MWC Faith and Life Commission.

became additional measurements of spiritual maturity, especially among some churches influenced by charismatic megachurch movements.

Bible reading, prayer, church ministries, and tithing are clearly important. But this paradigm of spiritual growth presumes that maturity in Christian faith can be achieved by programmable, artificial procedures. Driver, in turn, defines Christian spirituality as "the experience of every dimension of human life being oriented around and animated by the very Spirit of Jesus." Driver's discussions of spirituality thus focus on authentic humanity from a holistic perspective. Following the hermeneutic paradigm of the Anabaptists of the sixteenth century, Driver reveals that the cross of Jesus was the center of identity and experience for first-century Christians. The Beatitudes specifically indicate the spiritual quality of the messianic community.

For Driver, Christian spirituality is the lifelong process of following Jesus, starting from the baptismal confession of our willingness to imitate Jesus' sacrificial love, reconfirmed in the Lord's Supper, and continued by pursuing the justice and peace of the kingdom of God in our everyday lives.

Spirituality has to be embodied within a faith community. The lives of the disciples in the world, but not of the world, inevitably encounter hardship and difficulties. Yet Christian spirituality must be missional because the very nature of discipleship is living for others.

The twenty-first century has been called the post-modern era, emphasizing communities, paradigms, and narratives. Anabaptism, however, has embodied communitarianism for five hundred years because of its congregation-oriented theological approach. Given that the church is the masterpiece of the grace of the triune God, Anabaptists must listen to insights on the Holy Spirit and the Trinity within the global church, anticipating that there will always be something more that goes beyond our expectations.

In addition, current research in fields such as cultural anthropology and religious psychology can help improve our understanding of the edification of character, the nature of religious experiences, or the construction of community identity, and serve to deepen our theological reflections on spirituality.

For the Chinese churches, which have been deeply influenced by individualistic theological traditions and yet are located within a group-oriented social context, Driver powerfully identifies the significance of the communal aspect of Christian salvation experiences – salvation is not only individual, but also communal. Justification should not be separated from sanctification because both are corporate experiences of the church.

In the same way, spirituality is both personal and communal. Every individual experiences it differently, yet it reflects the same church experience. Accordingly, right teaching and right practice go hand in hand; theology and ethics illuminate one another. Both are edified in the faith community. Chinese usually value virtues, looking for the holistic harmony among heaven, humanity, nature, and self. Driver's theological unification of spirituality, church, and mission seems relevant to the Chinese context. A new paradigm emerges from Driver's discourse – everyday life can be a spiritual exercise. Christian spirituality is forged in daily life, in the communal experience of those who are in the world but not of the world.

The Spirit of Our Spirituality

Patricia Urueña Barbosa

Many have emphasized that we are living in the age of spiritualities. People today are drawn to finding a type of spirituality that will satisfy them and bring meaning and peace to their lives. In his book, *Life Together in the Spirit,* John Driver focuses on the theme of Christian spirituality from an Anabaptist perspective. Driver describes Christian spirituality as a holistic experience that is lived out "in all dimensions of life." Moreover, he understands such spirituality to be incarnated in history: "God's people imitate God – that is, they follow Jesus and they live out the communion of the Spirit – in all dimensions of life, both personal and corporate." At the same time, he invites us to let ourselves be guided by the Spirit of God – to live our spirituality within the committed community, pursuing a way of life that is consistent with what we believe while transforming situations of oppression, injustice, poverty, exclusion, and violence. In this we are in agreement. Our understanding of spirituality is determined by our conception of the church, God, Jesus, and the Holy Spirit, and should be lived in a consistent manner within

Patricia Urueña Barbosa of Columbia founded a Mennonite Church in Quito, Ecuador with her husband César Moya. She is active in the Latin American Women Doing Theology movement.

our diverse social, religious, economic, political, and cultural contexts.

Now, if, guided by the Spirit, we take a step back from what Driver says, in order to continue building our present and future, a question arises before us: How well do we know this Spirit that governs our spirituality?

Throughout history people have tried to explain the "mystery" of the Spirit of God – what it is or who it is, what it does or how it acts. When we talk about God, what we are doing is describing God from what we know, from our sometimes subjective experience. We might look at the universe and say, "What perfection! God is all in all, the Creator." When we receive the love that our parents offer us, we connect it to the love of God and think, "God loves us as a good father or mother would." This occurs constantly in our experience of trying to understand God. The biblical writers – those who wrote and taught about the Spirit of God as they interpreted their lived experience – also did this, with full certainty and faith that God had intervened in their history and the history of humankind. To describe these experiences of faith they used narratives with symbols and images in their worship celebrations, expressing their praise to God.

By images of God, I do not mean paintings, sculptures, or printed images of Jesus or the Holy Spirit, but expressions that are used to understand or explain God. When we use the image of God as father, for example, we imply that God conceived us, cares for us, provides all that we need, and loves us. But this is not the only image we have of God. There are other images of God that we find in the Bible: savior, source of life, our shield, refuge, rock, and many more. Just one expression or image of God is not sufficient to explain all of God. On the contrary, each image or expression of God is best complemented by others. One holistic image of God appearing in the wisdom tradition of the Old Testament is the image of the Spirit of God or the Wisdom of God (known as *Sophia* in the New Testament); it is a good image for understanding how the Spirit of God acts in the Word.

In biblical wisdom literature we also find abundant sources for talking about the action of the Holy Spirit. Surprisingly, Hebrew terms related to the Spirit of God are grammatically feminine: *shekinah* (the presence of God); *ruah* (spirit, its Greek equivalent is the gender-neutral *pneuma*); and *hokmah* (wisdom, *sophia* in Greek, also feminine). The Hebrew Scriptures use *hokmah* to talk about the mystery of God using feminine symbols; it is the biblical figure of Wisdom and the personification of the presence and activity of God in the Old Testament. *Ruah* is used to talk about the presence of the Spirit, alluding to God as a powerful creator and liberator in the world. Scripture associates the term *shekinah* with the Spirit of God, signaling God's permanent presence among the people of Israel. Therefore one form, although not the only one, that is found in the Old Testament to describe the tender, maternal, loving, caring action of God among God's people is the image of the Spirit of God. According to Proverbs 3:19 and 8:23–31, the Spirit existed since before the creation of the universe, actively participating in the gestation, organizing, ordering, and sustaining of creation. The Spirit delights in the wonder of creation and enjoys being present among humankind. Proverbs 8:1–12, in turn, recognizes the presence and activity of God through the personification of Wisdom. This is made evident wherever public life happens – on the journey, at the crossroads, when we don't know where we are going.

This Spirit calls us to live lives committed to truth, justice, and peace. The Spirit of Wisdom guides God's people to discover what it means to live a righteous life and walk in its paths. In Proverbs 1:20–21 and 9:1–6 she raises her voice in public places, calling together those who wish to listen. She looks for people in the street and invites them to her banquet table. She saves those she finds along the way. Her home is the cosmos that has no walls. She delights in all that has been created and cares for it. Her table is prepared for all. Wisdom sends out her prophets and apostles to call all people together – including those who are in the street – so that they may find truth, learn justice, become wise, and become friends of God.

Wisdom's banquet table provides food and drink for our daily struggles with the hope that we will become different people, forged into a different church and a world of justice, equality, and well-being. This does not mean we are to be idealistic dreamers. Rather, the table gathers together women and men who, in the power of the Spirit, seek to actualize the vision of God's alternative community, society, and reality – justice and well-being for all, including the well-being of creation.

In this way the Old Testament, through the Spirit, teaches about the presence of God and the Spirit's participation in the created order, assuring us of God's presence in history and in the life of God's people. The attributes that Judaism assigned to the Spirit of Wisdom, the New Testament writers assigned to Jesus, a point that deserves more extensive study.

We can conclude that our spirituality should be lived in a form consistent with our understanding of the Spirit of God. We should continue in its steps and accept the invitation of its prophets – to live our lives in communities committed to justice and truth; to form inclusive communities, because the table is prepared for all; and to dedicate ourselves to the well-being of all, including creation.

This is the Spirit that should determine our spirituality in contexts of exclusion and marginalization like those in which we live in the twenty-first century.

The Place of the Holy Spirit in Local Congregations

Nellie Mlotshwa

For decades the local Anabaptist churches in Zimbabwe have been very conservative and aloof regarding what John Driver calls "radical spirituality." Members dedicated themselves to the hard work of evangelism, prayer, Bible study, teaching, almsgiving, and discipleship. All these practices were believed to have been influenced and administered by the Holy Spirit. The Bible was considered to be the only standard measure for all matters of conscience and conduct. It was also believed to be consistently thorough and reliable in all matters of spirituality.

Since the beginning of the twenty-first century, however, worship styles in our local Anabaptist congregations have taken a new twist. Members have been debating, both formally and informally, the definition of true spirituality. Some claim to have manifestations of the gifts of the Spirit, particularly that of speaking in tongues. Others claim to have discovered a new dimension to their spirituality. Many have been carried away with the charisma involved in the worship styles of other denominations, insisting that true spirituality should be manifested through the gift of tongues. Others are claiming that their Christian orientation was too conservative

Nellie Mlotshwa, a church leader and theologian in Zimbabwe, has served as principal of Ekuphileni Bible Institute.

to allow for the current manifestations of the Spirit. "Something new has just dawned in the church," they claim. Changing worship styles and other new practices testify to the revolution that is currently taking place in our local congregations. Given these changes, genuine spirituality in our context might have different expressions than the one Driver describes in *Life Together in the Spirit*. The weakness in the current focus on speaking in tongues is a tendency to get carried away with one gift and thus downplay true spirituality, which embodies all the gifts of the Spirit and much more.

While I agree with Driver's basic line of reasoning, I think he should have emphasized more strongly, even for the ordinary Christian reader, the importance of an individual's decision for Christ. He needs to elaborate more on how one becomes part of the body of Jesus Christ and thus experiences the kind of spirituality Driver describes. I am aware that he explains in passing. It could be that his aim is to begin with the already existing body of Christ, disregarding the foundational stones on which it is built. But I consider the new birth to be foundational to true spirituality. People cannot become part of this body of Jesus Christ unless they start individually. In our case, this is where many miss the mark.

Jesus made sure that Nicodemus understood the crucial issue of the new birth, even as an individual. To become a participant in this beautiful journey, one needs to make an informed, individual U-turn from one's sins to accept

Christ. Having said this, I also want to acknowledge that only the Father draws people to Christ (John 6:44).

Other themes in the book connect well with our setting. Our circles, like Driver, would find it very difficult to accept the proposition of an abstract and obscure body of Jesus Christ. Driver taps into the Anabaptist definition of the true church as the concrete and visible body of Jesus Christ present in the world. This description aligns to some extent with that of Matthew 5:14.

Water baptism was of paramount importance as a public demonstration of the inner work of the Spirit. This line of thinking in Driver's book is noteworthy because many in our congregations do not realize that it is only a symbol or confirmation of the inner change of heart.

Driver's reference to the believers in the first century is very fitting to reinforce the argument for the oneness in the Spirit of the church of Jesus Christ. This community of believers in the early church set the pattern by demonstrating a life of togetherness in the spirit. They are a perfect example of the "people of the Way," as they were known. Those who lived together in one accord and freely shared their love and possessions are worth emulating.

Driver has also cited some recent examples of those who stood out and demonstrated a life of true spirituality, among them Mother Teresa. Her lifestyle was an example of "love in action"; her love could not be understood in abstract terms. Only "love in action" is true love and authentic spirituality. In our African setting, we value community. We are a people marked by a gregarious instinct, which should be the case in the body of Christ as well.

Issues of peace and justice need to be emphasized more, since our world is so prone to violence and divisions. As a peace church, we need to encourage peace and justice, reconciliation and forgiveness. True shalom is comprehensive. If we truly embraced shalom, it would bring a remarkable transformation to our communities.

Hopes for the Future

There is a bright hope for the Anabaptist church at large to rise to her full potential spiritually. Prayer and revival campaigns will give the members a vigorous shake-up to grasp the need for a spirituality that is not of their own making. The kind of spirituality anticipated is possible only through the enabling power of the Holy Spirit and a special touch from the Lord.

We hope fervently for tangible and positive results when the church embarks on well-structured teaching programs that clear some misconceptions concerning true spirituality and educate the church on matters of authentic spirituality. One can never fathom what God will do in response to sincere prayer and deep study of the Word. The Word is a true standard and blueprint for God's children to know what direction to take, whatever the circumstances.

The church depends on the Word which is "a lamp to their feet and a light to their path" (Ps. 119:105) to reach their goal. Without it they will only grope about in the dark. It is time our local church took a brave leap into the dark with the help of local Anabaptist Bible teachers to embark on an intensive Bible study. Whatever stumbling blocks might arise, the Lord will intervene and pave the way.

Another tool for the church to boost her hopes for the future is verbal communication. Thoughtful dialogue will go a long way to draw the members together for a common cause. The church needs to come together in a relaxed and friendly atmosphere to discuss whatever differences might exist among the members.

It is also important to move together as a body, like the believers of the first century, towards receiving the blessing of the Holy Spirit. For a dialogue to be successful, members need to tap into the church's primary strengths and experiences in matters of spirituality, while paying special attention to possible challenges and pitfalls that might lead to divisions due to differences of opinion on the question at hand. It is wise to maximize the willingness of the members to tackle issues together. The Holy Spirit will shed light only if the members pray together and keep their desire in the foreground, as did the first-century church.

Endnotes

1. See "A Vision for Global Mission Amidst Shifting Realities," *Anabaptist Witness* 1:1 (2014) and "The Relevance, Validity, and Urgency of Anabaptism for Our Time: Contemporary Ecclesiological Currents in Latin American Christianity," *The Mennonite Quarterly Review* 83:4 (Oct. 2014), 451–478.

2. Dorothee Soelle, *The Silent Cry: Mysticism and Resistance* (Minneapolis: Fortress Press, 2001).

3. David J. Bosch, *A Spirituality of the Road* (Scottdale, PA: Herald Press, 1979), 13–14.

4. Segundo Galilea, *El camino de la espiritualidad* (Buenos Aires: Paulinas, 1982), 41–44.

5. Walter Klaassen, *Anabaptism in Outline* (Scottdale, PA: Herald Press, 1981), 87.

6. Galilea, *El camino de la espiritualidad,* 59.

7. The principal biblical texts are Galatians 5:16–6:10 and Romans 8:1–30.

8. Hans Denck, the humanistically oriented South German radical reformer, as well as Ulrich Stadler, spokesman for the Austrian Hutterian Brethren, agree on this point: "I value Holy Scripture above all human treasures but not as high as the Word of God, which is living, powerful and eternal, and which is free and unencumbered by all the elements of this world. For insofar as it [the Word] is God himself it is spirit and no letter, written without pen and paper and it may never be expunged. Therefore also salvation cannot be tied to the Scriptures, however important and good they may be with respect to it." Klaassen, *Anabaptism in Outline,* 142.

    And further: "Therefore whoever wishes to use the Scripture with true reverence and not to attribute to it more than it deserves, or belongs to it, must radically separate the Scriptures and the spoken word from the inner word of the heart... [The outer word] is not the living Word of God but only a letter or likeness or witness of the inner or eternal Word. This living Word is internally witnessed by the outer word if one pays close attention to it. It is like a sign on an inn which witnesses to the wine in the cellar. But the sign is not the wine... The true inner Word is the eternal almighty power of God, of the same form in man as in God, which is capable of all things. It is given after perseverance in many tribulations in the discipline of the Lord. John calls this the new commandment that is true in him and in you. Only Christ under the holy cross teaches this. According to the true order of God this Word is preceded by the outer word. The preacher is to admonish by means of the external word that one should surrender and listen to the internal teacher and not allow the people to depend upon the outer word. Otherwise preachers, Scriptures, and words become idols." Ibid., 143, 145–146.

9. George H. Williams, *The Radical Reformation* (Philadelphia: Westminster Press, 1962), 823.

10. Cornelius J. Dyck, ed., *An Introduction to Mennonite History* (Scottdale, PA: Herald Press, 1967), 23.

11. The Donatists held that the church must be composed of saints and not sinners, and that baptisms conducted by bishops who were discovered to be traitors to the Christian cause were invalid. Augustine and the dominant Catholic tradition rejected these arguments, insisting that the purity of the church was ultimately in God's hands.

12. The following quotation is extracted from Luther's "Preface to the German Mass and Order of Service," written in 1526: "The third kind of service should be a truly evangelical order and should not be held in a public place with all sorts of people. But those who want to be Christians . . . should sign their names and meet alone in a house somewhere to pray, to read, to baptize, to receive the sacrament, and to do other Christians works. According to this order, those who do not lead Christian lives could be known, reproved, corrected, cast out, or excommunicated, according to the rule of Christ, Matthew 18 [:15–17]. Here one could also solicit benevolent gifts to be willingly given and distributed to the poor, according to St. Paul's example, 2 Corinthians 9. Here would be no need of much and elaborate singing. Here one could set up a brief and neat order for baptism and the sacrament and center everything on the Word, prayer, and love. . . . In short, if one had the kind of people and persons who wanted to be Christians in earnest, the rules and regulations would soon be ready. But as yet I neither can nor desire to begin such a congregation or assembly or to make rules for it. . . . For if I should try to make it up out of my own need, it might turn into a sect." Ulrich S. Leupold, ed., *Liturgy and Hymns, in Luther's Works*, ed. Helmut T. Lehmann (Philadelphia: Fortress Press, 1965), 53:62–64.

13. J. C. Wenger, ed., *The Complete Writings of Menno Simons,* trans. Leonard Verduin (Scottdale, PA: Herald Press, 1956), 739–741.

14. Klaassen, *Anabaptism in Outline,* 215.

15. Ibid., 191–192.

16. Ibid., 193.

17. John H. Yoder, trans. and ed., *The Legacy of Michael Sattler* (Scottdale, PA: Herald Press, 1973), 45.

18. Ibid., 45.

Endnotes

19. George H. Williams and Angel M. Mergal, eds., *Spiritual and Anabaptist Writers* (Philadelphia: The Westminister Press, 1957), 73–74.

20. Ibid., 79.

21. Ibid., 80.

22. Yoder, *The Legacy of Michael Sattler*, 39–41.

23. Ibid., 70–71.

24. Ibid., 72–73.

25. Cornelius J. Dyck, *Spiritual Life in Anabaptism* (Scottdale, PA: Herald Press, 1995), 113.

26. Ibid., 114.

27. Ibid., 116.

28. Ibid., 119.

29. Ibid., 123.

30. It is interesting to note that this text was also among those most quoted by Christian writers of the first three centuries.

31. Conrad Grebel compared parts of the singing in the cathedral in Zurich to the "barking of dogs."

32. C. Arnold Snyder, *From Anabaptist Seed* (Intercourse, PA: Good Books, 1999), 5, 46.

33. Yoder, *The Legacy of Michael Sattler,* 36, 38.

34. Wenger, *Complete Writings of Menno Simons,* 558.

Related titles from Plough

The Early Christians
Eberhard Arnold

Salt and Light
Eberhard Arnold

God's Revolution
Eberhard Arnold

Discipleship
J. Heinrich Arnold

Jesus and the Nonviolent Revolution
André Trocmé

Everyone Belongs to God
Christoph Friedrich Blumhardt

*Using this book in a discussion group? Contact
Plough for quantity discounts.*

Plough Publishing House
www.plough.com
1-800-521-8011 ▪ 845-572-3455
PO BOX 398 ▪ Walden, NY 12586 ◆ USA
Brightling Rd ▪ Robertsbridge ▪ East Sussex TN32 5DR ▪ UK
4188 Gwydir Highway ▪ Elsmore, NSW 2360 ▪ Australia